MW01204175

Jazz Idiom

Keep the Beat Steady and Enjoy!

Jazz

Jazz Idiom
BLUEPRINTS, STILLS AND FRAMES

THE JAZZ PHOTOGRAPHY OF
CHARLES L. ROBINSON

POETIC TAKES AND RIFFS BY
AL YOUNG

BAYTREE

Heyday Books, Berkeley, California
BAYTREE BOOKS

Copyright © 2008 by Charles L. Robinson and Al Young

This book was made possible in part by a generous grant from the BayTree Fund.

All rights reserved. No portion of this work may be reproduced or transmitted in any form or by any means, electronic or mechanical, including photocopying and recording, or by any information storage and retrieval system, without permission in writing from Heyday Books.

Library of Congress Cataloging-in-Publication Data

Robinson, Charles L.
Jazz idiom : blueprints, stills, and frames : the jazz photography of Charles L. Robinson / photographs and comments by Charles L. Robinson ; poetic takes and riffs by Al Young.
p. cm. -- (BayTree books)
Includes bibliographical references (p.   ).
ISBN-13: 978-1-59714-095-9 (pbk. : alk. paper)
1. Jazz musicians--United States--Portraits. 2. Jazz--Pictorial works. I. Young, Al, 1939- II. Title.
ML87.R625 2008
781.65092'273--dc22
2007047362

On the Cover: Carmen McRae

Design and Layout: theBookDesigners (bookdesigners.com)

Printed in Singapore by Imago

Orders, inquiries, and correspondence should be addressed to:
Heyday Books
P. O. Box 9145, Berkeley, CA 94709
(510) 549-3564, fax (510) 549-1889
www.heydaybooks.com

10 9 8 7 6 5 4 3 2 1

To the intensely committed teachers of Baltimore's Francis M. Wood

Elementary School for Handicapped Negro Children (Class of 1946), and

the similarly committed teachers of Paul Laurence Dunbar High School

(Class of 1951).

—*Charles L. Robinson*

C o n t e n t s

Personal Acknowledgments

To all the musicians and friends who tolerated (and respected)
my whistling, humming, and singing bebop and standards to them

In memory of
Merrill Hoover,
pianist to
Anita O'Day and
Mary Stallings,
and tutor to
many singers and other musicians

To my father,
who played a little piano, and exposed me to the music
of Baltimore's Pennsylvania Avenue clubs

To the live and recorded music of Duke Ellington,
Art Tatum, Stan Kenton, and others

To Martha, my first wife, for buying me an Argus C3
and starting me over again in photography

To Sarah, my current wife, who went with me on many an unpaid photo shoot

To the many writers on photography who provided the references for teaching me the
minutiae of getting quality from 35mm film, *e.g.*, the use of "nose grease" for negative
scratches, how to load cassettes from bulk rolls of 50 or 100 feet, and the pulling in of
elbows to your sides for slow shutter speeds

C L R

"The adage in Kansas City was and still is: *Say something on your horn*—don't just show off your versatility and ability to execute. *Tell us a story, and don't let it be a lie*. Let it *mean* something."

—*Gene Ramey, bassist*

Introduction

IT WAS SMACK DAB IN THE MIDDLE of 1962 that I—a folksinging writer and jazz dee-jay situated at the time in the middle of Berkeley—turned twenty-three. That was when I met Charles Robinson for the first time. The artist Glenn Myles, one of whose flamboyant pen and ink drawings would later illuminate a Taj Mahal album, intro-duced us. Right away, from jump, we liked one another. As music lovers and as geo-graphic transplants, we connected at once.

Everybody seemed to be up to something artistic or creative. I was playing guitar and singing in East Bay bars, clubs, and cof-feehouses: the Blind Lemon, the Cabale, the Jabberwock, and in San Francisco at the Coffee Gallery in North Beach and the Drinking Gourd on Union Street. I knew painters, sculptors, actors, dancers, poets, novelists, journalists, musicians, playwrights, filmmakers. Albert Johnson, future founder of the San Francisco Film Festival, lived upstairs; Stacy Keach, then unknown, used to visit as did Ernest "Chick" Callenbach, editor of *Film Quarterly,* who would later author the cult ecology classic *Ecotopia*. Upstairs, too, lived Dennis Allison, who would become a leading computer scientist and Silicon Valley visionary. My girlfriend's boss was Pauline Kael, who, with her husband, Ed Landberg, was running Telegraph Avenue's Cinema Guild and Studio, the nation's first repertory

13

movie house. As a volunteer best boy and gopher on low-budget and no-budget underground film crews, I had come to know many a stage- or screen-struck character.

In times that were heavy, the youthful mood was heady. The music scene was in a boil. My generation had experienced music as popular song (ballads, standards, show tunes; Irving Berlin, George and Ira Gershwin, Duke Ellington, Cole Porter, Rodgers and Hart, Johnny Mercer), dance music, big band swing, small band bebop, blues, rhythm and blues, and doo-wop. You could hole up in this stately house of music and safeguard yourself, but you couldn't drown out the sound of rock and roll, which was kicking down the door. Everything was changing. *Change of the Century* was the title that plastic-sax jazz adventurer Ornette Coleman had given his critically heralded 1959 album. The San Francisco Bay Area—already world-renowned as a cradle for cultural craziness, a haven for the offbeat— jumped and seethed with music and art.

When it came to the graphic arts, I already knew a whole lot of avid picture-takers. Charles Robinson was no picture-taker; he was a photographer, a truly contemplative photographer. Several years my senior, he had made the move ten years previously from Maryland to California, from urban Baltimore to agricultural Vallejo. He lived there with an aunt while he attended college prep courses at Vallejo Junior College, where he didn't let a polio-affected leg keep him off the swimming team. One of his classmates, a track star in those days, was Louisiana-born Ernest J. Gaines, now celebrated for his best-selling novels and short stories. As I, the fledgling poet-novelist, began to swim upstream in the literary sea, Gaines befriended and encouraged me. "In Vallejo," he said, "my family was out there in the bean fields, struggling. I wanted to write. At San Francisco State, I read Chekhov, Pushkin, Turgenev, the Russians who wrote about their peasantry and underdogs. I realized my people were black southern peasants. I wanted to write about that. I wanted to write about my people."

"My people, I suspect," Charles Robinson let me know, "had sent me out to California to be with my aunt. My grandmother had died. But I think they wanted to get me away from those numbers people in Baltimore. I'd already been tapped on the shoulder. They were waiting for me to get out of high school. And the guys in the barbershop had anointed me. The thing that saved my life was my mother had agreed with my aunt that

I would come out here and live with her.

"It's hard to modestly tell folks what your experience is, and to have them receive it modestly. Because automatically they think you're bragging when, in fact, the coincidences said I had to do this in order to survive. I'm not talking about life and death, but to have money in my pocket. Even the job right after high school in a women's dress shop—eleven dollars a week, six days. That pay was so low that they didn't take out income tax. Somehow I got word of a job in a British men's clothing store, Eddie Jacobs in downtown Baltimore, for thirteen dollars, for the same six days. The guy hired me, man. I mean, jumping jobs for two dollars.

"But I also know that if I'd stayed in Baltimore, I wasn't going to college, and I wouldn't be alive now. Or I'd be in some dead-end job, something that'd keep me on my feet, so I'd wear out my one good leg.

"There are a bunch of positive things about coming to California. So many unbelievable experiences! They just happened. Writing a swimming column for the [San Francisco] *Sun Reporter,* writing the jazz column for the *Golden Gater* (San Francisco State's paper), getting the Modern Jazz Quartet to come to San Francisco State to do a noon concert for a dollar. Having been a Boy Scout, I got the Boy Scout Alumni Association to do all the grunt work, handle tickets and so forth. It really was a fundraiser for them. I couldn't have pulled that off five years later, or even three years later. The status that came from being the writer of *Jazz Idiom*, the name of my SF State column.

"At the same time, I was working as a Red Cross water safety instructor for the Oakland Recreation Department in the summertime. Also, I was working as a house father at Edgewood Orphanage in San Francisco. This started during my last year as an undergraduate, before I went into grad school. This happened because I was in vocational rehabilitation counseling. When the psychologist interviewed me, I was perfect, because they had enough minority kids in the place who were emotionally disturbed. So they wanted somebody of color. So I had a job with meals included with some money, and they did your laundry for you, too. I couldn't ask for anything more.

"I was also tied in with this attorney, a good friend, Dick Wertheimer. He was a post-polio guy I had met in Vallejo. We became lifelong friends. He was the one who was going to subsidize the book I wanted to do. You remember the movie *Don't Look Back,* on Bob Dylan? There was a paperback book with stills from that film. I wanted to do a similar book on Duke Ellington. Dick was going to pay for my travel and my expenses for that one month of shooting. The unfortunate thing was that Ralph Gleason and KQED-TV were doing *their* documentary on Duke. When I talked about it with Mercer, Duke's son who had come back to the band and was now road manager, I offered him ten percent of the royalties. Mercer said, 'I'll need that ten percent up front.' So I walked away from it.

"Collectively, with stuff like that just happening—when you look back at it, it's almost unbelievable, man. Ernest Dunbar on the editorial staff of *Look* magazine who was trying to boost me. Ted and Shirley Streshinsky because they wanted the 'honor' of promoting me as their 'new Gordon Parks.' Which was kind of fun, but I wasn't going to leave town on no humbug, man. No way. Not with two kids to take care of.

"All of that long-windedness is to point out how post-polios can be labeled over-achievers because of the different things they get into. Also, like most people with orthopedic problems, I wanted to be a doctor, an orthopedist. My undergraduate degree was in biology. What I didn't know is that medical school is almost a cinch—that is, if you've got a mentor. And "mentor" means a whole lot of things: come up with the money, piggyback on whatever school they came from, etcetera. So that didn't work out.

"Serendipity. I lucked up. My advisor at SF State was in the Phys Ed department. By this time I was talking about becoming a physical therapist. She was advisor for pre–physical therapy people, which was a one-year program at UC Med School. She told me about this vocational rehabilitation program that was just coming brand new in 1957. The government was giving stipends to beef up the occupation and get people in it. I enrolled in the program. For three semesters I was the only one in the program without a stipend. But since I already had this house-father job at Edgewood that paid $200 a month, I didn't really need the money.

"That's how I got into the rehab thing and, as you know, I was always interested in the music part. I brought back this interest in photography. Martha, my first wife, for a birthday present, bought me this camera: an Argus C3. The nickname for it was The Brick. That's when I started back in photography. Charlie Sykes and I grew up together. His father was a dentist—in fact, his father was a pitcher for the Black Sox. Charlie had a sink in his third-floor bedroom. His brother taught us how to develop film. His brother had a twin-lens reflex camera. There were a whole bunch of Rolleiflex copycats. We took pictures of one another. That's my beginning as far as photography is concerned. Unless you got money, you don't get into photography. You got to buy too much.

"One guy I admire is Erich Salomon, who was taking pictures candidly with available light since World War I. He was hiding his camera under his coat because photography was *verboten*. He's the hero of the early photojournalists, including Cartier-Bresson. No flash, so you preserve the integrity of the scene—I still stand by this."

The arrival of his son, Joseph, in 1963 and his daughter, Sybil, in 1965 deepened Charles' practical and responsible side. Popular standup comic Chris Rock might very well have in mind Charles Robinson when he says, "There's a lot of black fathers that handle their stuff, brothers who take care of business." Following his graduation from San Francisco State University, he worked for the State of California as a counselor for the Department of Rehabilitation, then as an office manager for the Human Resources Development Department. "As a photographer," he confides, "I never had to hustle. I always had my day job to fall back on."

—

THAT TWO OF HIS FAVORITE ARTISTS are the Dutch painter Johannes Vermeer and the French photographer Henri Cartier-Bresson reveals much about Charles L. Robinson's artistic ethics and horizons. Having come of age in the grand era of such popular publications as *Life*, *Look*, *Quick*, *Paris-Match*, *Época*, *Ebony*, and *Jet*, he has been a lifelong student and follower of photojournalism. He fondly recalls how the *The Christian Science Monitor*, when it was a full-sized daily, used to run one entire page of photos in its weekend edition. "One photographer in particular shot everyday stuff," Charles explains. "A mother with two children, say, grocery shopping. That's what I like about good photojournalism. It caught the exceptional in everyday life. It wasn't staged." Robinson champions what Henri Cartier-Bresson termed "the decisive moment." And, as it had with Cartier-Bresson, the 35mm camera became "an extension of the eye."

Of course there is a sense in which all artists are journalists. From its beginnings in the early nineteenth century, photography has always captured more than meets the picture-taking eye. As it is possible to get a firm idea of bourgeois values in the 1600s by looking at Vermeer's sumptuously

17

detailed interiors of household life in the Dutch Golden Age, so it is possible to pore over Robinson's many pictures of Duke Ellington and note that in one particular shot the great composer-pianist, inexplicably, is sporting a jacket unbefitting his royal standards. This is the musician whom Stevie Wonder called "the King of All, Sir Duke." What was going on with His Jazz Majesty that afternoon, that evening, that morning?

Time and space, light and sound—all of these mysteries feed the love that comes down between photographer and subject, devotee and icon. And when the devotee is a lifelong music lover whose icon is jazz, breathe easy. At any celebration of jazz graphics or iconography, my friend Charles can come early and stay late. A man of playful spirit, he takes his photographs seriously.

"There are a lot of people who want to be participants in something. Not satisfied with the vicarious kind of participation of, you know, listening, they want more. What I've noticed in recent years is that photographers, photographers particularly, have to be on stage with the performers. I'm insulted by that. They're not part of the act. They justify it because a lot of them are video-photographers; they need the angle of view, or whatever. They get in with the band. I'm insulted because it's distracting, especially if it's not some rote performance, but a creative process is going on. It's more than that fifteen minutes of fame thing; everybody wants to be on stage, to be performers of some kind or to have people watching them.

"With respect to my own attitude, philosophy, I claim guilty to some kind of vicariousness from the standpoint of I love the music. Years ago I discovered it was too late to try to develop competency on a particular instrument in order to express myself musically. I tried taking piano lessons. Unfortunately, I didn't have a keyboard at home to come right home and practice. The teacher was disappointed. She thought I was running a scam of some kind. I knew a lot about the feeling of music and would tell her about it in the context of jazz. She kept testing me, saying things like, 'And what instrument did you play?' She didn't believe me when I told her I *didn't* play. What I was telling her was stuff I had intellectually absorbed. She was surprised that I could read music. I told her, 'Well, I taught myself to read music. I took a music appreciation class, but I did that forty years ago.' There were and are all kinds of references around to help you read stuff. Obviously, like anything else, if you don't stay at it you don't develop any speed. For me it was a chance to appreciate the artistry, the creativeness involved in being a musician.

"Being visually oriented seems like a contradiction. I tried drawing a little bit, cartoons. It was a way of connecting, even with musicians. It was a way of being up close and intimate, even in a way, I discovered, that jazz critics and writers couldn't be. Okay? It had something to do with my ethnicity, exploiting the positiveness of that. If I'd been a white photographer, being in the room with Art Blakey and Billy Eckstine—who are old friends—their conversation would've been different. I was flattered by that. They didn't challenge me at all about taking their pictures and their gestures, which was a perfect environment for a photographer.

"The music teacher kept asking me, 'Why didn't you play by ear?' Well, my daddy played by ear. Somehow or other, I didn't see the legitimacy—I don't know how else to define it—of not being able to read. To be able to hear the stuff is very frightening and satisfying at the same time. Of course I can hear a lot more now than I could fifty years ago: the harmony, where it ought to go, or where it *could* go. To feel how something…

Even the hum of a pedal point, that pitch. To know that it's right is very exciting.

"My interest in photography springs from the music. The music was always in the neighborhood I grew up in. Someone on [Bay Area FM jazz station] KCSM was talking about Cannonball Adderley and how he and his brothers had their degrees, and they were musicians in New York. Other musicians and fans were suspicious of them because they were teachers, educators, and whatever church denomination they belonged to was rigid; they didn't even get to hear blues in the house. In a black neighborhood…the church across the street from me had one door with a tin sheet over it. You could hear music on Tuesday night. It was a church; they had evening sessions. You heard it. That's all there was to it. Music itself was so much a basic part of your environment that even if you weren't a musician you still had music in your life, even if you didn't have it in your house. It was so much a part of you— Lloyd Glenn's "Chick-a-Boo," which I came to love, stayed on that jukebox in the pool hall, man, for a year. I mean, the guy who came weekly to collect money from the jukebox and put records in, he had to come and put a new record in. They wore it out.

19

"My whole idea, as far as taking pictures was concerned, my whole thing was to study the artist first. If they had particular moves that fit with their style—whether they were instrumentalists or singers—I would try to capture that visually.

"There are certain singers, like Anita O'Day, who would *hold* a pose."

"On Bunny Briggs," he tells me, "I have to say this." Charles is referring to the great jazz tap dancer whom Ellington chose to perform in the very first of his sacred jazz concerts, staged at San Francisco's Grace (Episcopal) Cathedral in September of 1965. "David Danced Before the Lord with All His Might" is the title Ellington borrowed from II Samuel 6:14, which describes how King David danced before the Ark of the Covenant as it arrived in Jerusalem, the kingdom's new capital.

"I just found a DVD of the concert at Grace Cathedral, the original. I never made it to that concert, and I'm glad I didn't, because of all the complaints about the quality of the sound, and the echoes. The recording's all right. But to see Bunny Briggs make his moves, and remembering him from Monterey and how the musicians, they all watched him—the emotionality of his dancing, his playing! It was almost

like the way baseball players look at Ichiro Suzuki of the Seattle Mariners when he comes up to bat. Any baseball players with any sense, they watch Ichiro. That's the way musicians looked at Bunny Briggs.

"Now, taking a still of a dancer," Charles continues, "if I'm shooting with available light—and to this day I never want to interrupt or insult a scene with flash—the first thing I do is study and observe. Does he have some pattern to when he stops, when he's actually frozen? Then I have to anticipate this. The other thing I want to do is show the emotion. So in this sequence I shot of him, I intentionally wanted one of the last frames to be blurred, actively showing motion.

"I've established who Bunny Briggs is, shown the musicians watching him, entranced by him. The expression on his face—I didn't do a good job of catching that because, even though he's made a move, his whole body is in it. And so I'm very conscious of seeing what his pattern is, seeing if I can catch something that freezes it as much as I can with the low light, at the slow shutter speed. If he had a spotlight on him, then I could technically go to the 1/250th of a second."

"Jazz," Charles says, "allows you to come

in at so many different levels. Let's say you come in with the Horace Silver percussive-rhythmic thing, and you hang in there [with him] long enough that you get to know the performer. From that point on, you can always upgrade your ability to appreciate what's going on. Take, for example, [bassist] Ray Brown. I'm always excited by his intonation. I can tell today, when I hear Ray Brown. The gut strings, the wood of the bass. It's touch. Unlike some of the young guys who came after him, Ray was never out to show you how fast he was. Ray Brown's tone and the sound of his instrument—that *was* his touch. I'm curious today about who got his bass, and if anyone could get anywhere close to him. It's just beautiful to hear his grace notes. Tone, tone—that's all I can keep saying about Ray Brown."

"It's interesting," I tell Charles, "to consider what tone means in photography, and what it means in sound. Don't you think?"

"Hey, yeah, right," he laughs with a bass-like groan. "I have to tell you, man. I've cried listening to Ray Brown just keeping time. Not soloing. As a matter of fact, the stuff he plays—not always double-stops, where he's showing off some symphonic technique—it's just a fixed beat. And when you watch him, you don't see him working hard. And there's another bass player who just died, who was just as relaxed and who almost had the same speed. I know he studied Ray Brown. Danish dude. He worked with Oscar Peterson. Niels Ørsted Pedersen. I mean, I couldn't watch him when he was a youngster; I was busy taking pictures. But to study his technique—he gets the same speed as Ray, but not the same tone. I wondered if he ever played Ray Brown's bass. I suspect he had, but I just never heard it."

Of the friendly shot he snapped of Modern Jazz Quartet legends Milt Jackson and Connie Kay conversing with Dizzy Gillespie, Charles says: "As I recall it, that shot shows a camaraderie. It's implicit in their gestures, even though that suit is a little tight on Dizzy."

"Was that a style, or what?" I ask, descending into that conversational trivia zone where jazz crazies love to linger.

"What?"

"Wearing clothes too tight," I say. "You look at early pictures of [producer] Norman Granz, and his pants are hitting him way up the leg, his coat sleeves are too short, and he did that Ben Webster thing: his hat is too small."

"Oh, yeah." Charles laughs. "Actually, Granz didn't do it like Ben Webster. Ben

Webster's hat *sat* on his head. Granz pulled his hat down on his head; it was closer to Lester Young's. To me, based on my experience of working in a men's store, that suit of Norman Granz's was just too small."

"But, Charles, was that a fashion statement, or what? Why did Dizzy, who was fashion conscious…"

"Well, Dizzy was getting fatter, too. But the expression of those two guys, their faces, you could tell, man, there was some brotherly stuff there. They had just said something. Whatever it was, they'd clearly, emotionally communicated. They had mutually turned one another on. It's like using just one word, and you could tell this wasn't the first time they'd communicated with one another. This was what was so exciting. But I can't tell you I saw this before I took the picture. I'm sure I didn't see it until after I had printed it."

Jazz, of course, holds the key to savoring what photographer Robinson offers. If we knew nothing else about jazz aside from the fact that Charles has lived close to it all of his life, this would almost be enough to fully appreciate these artists he has fixed and preserved in shadow and light with such visible affection. It isn't until we remember that sound and silence are the auditory equivalent of shadow and light that we begin to appreciate and, more reliably, *feel* Robinson's achievement.

While I have spent a lifetime immersed in reflections about moments noticed, recorded moments—sound recordings, snapshots, home movies, home video, and don't get me started about notebooks—I'm often still startled by jazz-distilled photography. When once I asked a painter friend why black-and-white depictions often captivate us more than richly colored ones, she didn't miss a beat. She said, "Color does all the work for us. Black-and-white leaves plenty of room for us to imagine, to fill in stuff that isn't really spelled out. Think about it."

In the twenty years I've had to think about what she said, I've gone back and soaked up Charles Robinson's prints of his black-and-white portraits and informal studies. Sometimes I even see them as blueprints; that is, as a design for making something else. But what? A life in jazz or the performing arts, perhaps. Heavily infused with the blues as well as jubilance, jazz sometimes sounds and feels like a scaled-down model of life to me. Never forgetting that the very word photography comes from two Greek words: *photo* (light) and *graph* (write, sketch, draw, delineate), I like to believe that what poets do with words and silence, photographers accomplish with light and shadow. Whether writing with language or with light, artists must inevitably bear in mind that impressions, depictions, and sketches of people, things, and situations are not in themselves the actual people and things and situations that command or demand our attention. Relationships—that's what this artful fuss and muss is about.

—

AS IT HAPPENS, the late pop music columnist and jazz historian Ralph J. Gleason figured significantly into each of our lives. It was Gleason who introduced me to producer Orrin Keepnews after the two of them settled into their offices at Tenth and Parker Streets, home of Fantasy Prestige Milestone, the multi-labeled record company for which I would begin writing album liner notes in the 1970s. It was also during this period that Gleason stated in his *San Francisco Chronicle* column that the history of jazz was locked up in these surviving players' heads. Mentioning me by name in the column, Gleason also told me personally, "It's going to take someone like you to unlock their stories. As a black man, you'll get more out of them than I can. They'll tell you different stories than they tell me."

When I related to Charles Robinson what Gleason had told me shortly before he died, the unpredictable camera man said, "Yes, Ralph *made* them hire me at Monterey. It coincided with their staff photographer Jerry Stoll leaving. Jerry was starting to do films."

How Charles found time to work this new gig into his other activities I can barely imagine. At the time, the mid-1960s, he was a supervising rehabilitation counselor for the State of California, and board member and president of South Berkeley's Housing Development Corporation. He was also on the advisory board of SATE (Self-Advancement Through Education), which had begun as a self-help program for African American inmates at San Quentin. "Way back then," Charles says, "I was beginning to develop ideas about lateral thinking and problem-solving techniques." Still, as busy as he sometimes found himself, Charles Robinson has always been ardently devoted to family; he never neglected his wife, nor his son and daughter.

Organization is one of Charles' secrets. Just as he can readily retrieve memories of his childhood in Baltimore, so Charles can zero in on a particular item squirreled away in the vast and ever-growing archive of treasured recordings, books,

23

photographs, and clippings in his vibrant East Bay home. Once, when I told him I'd been assigned to write the liner notes for a reissue CD of the great Jimmy Smith's *Organ Grinder's Swing*, Charles said, "I might can help you out. I've got a file on Hammond organ players stashed away in my basement. Give me a couple of days. I'll find it and give it to you." To my delight, he did just that, and it didn't take him long. That "file" is "life" spelled inside out has never been wasted on the poet in me.

—

I LOVE THE WAY CHARLES' EYES TWINKLE, and the way his whole face beams when he tells these stories of what it was like to be on the set, as it were. Always dead set on letting life play or play out in its zigzag fashion, he is forever on friendly terms with that basic life-unit: the moment. While he has never been one to immerse himself in an abstract discussion or rant on the nature of time, Charles Robinson's understanding of the sanctity of the moment seems to override any notions about holiness that formal religion might have passed down to him. Like the legendary Billie Holiday, Charles is a Baltimore Catholic. "But we could hear. We were hip to what was going on at the Baptist and the African Methodist churches, too. I mean, it was all happening in the same neighborhood."

It's clear to any attentive still-photographer or photojournalist that everything happens in the moment. Analog or digital, pictures break down into frames. Frames of mind play a huge role as well. Unlike the fawning or predatory paparazzo, who stalks celebrities to shoot candid, bankable shots, photographers of Charles' persuasion respect their subjects' privacy. Henri Cartier-Bresson defined the "decisive moment" as "the simultaneous recognition, in a fraction of a second, of the significance of an event, as well as the precise organization of forms which gives that event its proper expression." In the presence of the celebrated—Muhammad Ali, James Brown, Louis Armstrong, renowned *Life* photographer Eugene Smith, cellist/political activist Pablo Casals—Charles Robinson never sells his convictions downriver. Like Cartier-Bresson, he believes that dignity, compassion, and love will always trump technique and brilliance, when it comes to taking a meaningful picture. Sometimes this may mean not shooting at all.

"There was another situation around Louis Armstrong. When I went with the guys to pick up Louis at the airport near Monterey, they had a bus waiting for him and the band. I went up into that bus and stood at the driver's seat and took pictures of Louis as he came up the steps. I had at least three cameras around me. He was the first one on the bus. Everybody else hung back.

"It was just the two of us. Louis went and took a seat on the aisle, and I took a picture. He had his glasses on, and he had a lot of correction in the lenses of his glasses, of course. And he said to me, 'Pops is a little tired now. Would you mind not taking any more pictures?' I had a strap on my camera, so I just let it drop out of my hands. I said, 'For you, Pops.'

"The integrity issue here is, I know photographers who would've said yes to Louis Armstrong, and then would've tried to sneak in some shots of him relaxing. That kind of ethic popped into my head. I said, 'There's no way that I would try to take a picture of him after he asked me *not* to, and I agreed not to.'"

At a moment when public officials and agencies seem determined to make documentary photography all but illegal, a moment when the nanosecond (one-billionth of a second) has become standard time-measure on an unreflective planet wobbling toward self-destruction, what pleasure it gives me to gaze at and ponder Charles' meaningful interactions with musicians whose work he admired, loved, or revered. Long on memory and bottomless on passion and concern, Charles Robinson is a treasure and a joy. What a pleasure and honor it is for me to play (I almost said *work*) with him in preparing this lasting collection of his heartfelt and lovingly made photographs.

Al Young
California Poet Laureate
April 2008

PHOTOGRAPHER'S NOTE

These few photos were done during the 1969–1972 period. Locations were: Monterey Jazz Festival; UC Berkeley, Zellerbach Hall; Mount Tamalpais, Marin County, California; Basin Street West, San Francisco; and Railroad Crossing, Berkeley.

—
C L R

SHOTS & TAKES | Stories & Riffs

Sounded, the name alone speaks out, speaks out. In bold poems, unworded but braided,
Monk counted off his melodies. And if you called him by his rightful name,
he smiled. If you called him Mister Monk, he glowed with dignity.
Monk-think zigzagged all through jazz to snag
just enough from its originators to make himself heard.

Thelonious Monk

1917–1982

I asked Monk if he would pose for me. He said okay. I was amazed. I mean, this was a guy who was used to people asking him stuff. He was used to putting people on, too. I know it had a lot to do with the way I asked him. But he posed for me. You can tell by the hat he was wearing what period it was. This was his LBJ hat. This was at Monterey. I had the print framed and Art Auerbach, who owned the Jazz Workshop, put it up on the wall there. Then we blew it up and put it just inside the door of the Workshop, right inside at the entrance. Monk used to go outside on Broadway when it was break time, between sets. "T," I said, "What do you think of that picture?" "What picture?" he said. I said, "Aw, come on, T!" So we stepped out there on Broadway. The club door was open. You could see the portrait. "So what do you think, T?" He was grinding his teeth. He laughed and said, "That's nice."

Duke Ellington

1899–1974

Why, Sir Duke, did you spend so much time sitting up all night,
writing music until dawn, making all those gigs and trotting the globe when you could've kicked back
and retired on your massive song royalties?
At the height of the Great Depression your royalty earnings ran close to one million dollars a year.
Ballads, suites, epics, ballet, opera, what didn't you undertake?

How did it feel to have to fire Mingus after he and Juan Tizol, your beloved saxophonist, got in a fight?
Puerto Rico–born, Tizol had written the classic "Perdido,"
whose title in English means "Lost." Your New Mexico–born, thin-skinned,
deep-thinking bass player hauled out a fire axe on Tizol, and Tizol a machete.
"Tizol is an old problem," you had to tell Mingus. "Why don't you resign? You're a new problem."

In one of your rare lyrics, you say:
"There's two kinds of woman, / Two kinds of man. / Two kinds of romance since time began. /
There's real true love, / And that good old jive. / One tries to kill you, / One helps to keep you alive. /
I don't know what kind of blues I've got." America's most prolific and terrific composer,
you did love us madly after all, didn't you?

Charles Mingus

1922–1979

MDM"—that's what you titled one of your lesser-played
ones, Mingus. It stood for Monk-Duke-Mingus, and
in it you spelled out in musical collage the melodic,
harmonic, and rhythmic debt you young player-
composers owed to the master. Seeing the notes on
paper wasn't the same as hearing, then sounding them.
While you were looking, you stopped and you listened.

Composition-wise, let me tell you one thing
I had in mind. The drum is symbolic—
that drum, on the left-hand side. Without
the drum, we don't even have jazz. So
the drum leads us into the filming of
this composition about a band rehearsal.
In his own band at the time, which featured Lonnie
Hillyer on trumpet and Charles McPherson on alto, the
nickname for Mingus was Da Ming.

Anita had her moves. When she made them, I was there.

Anita O'Day

1919–2006

When jazz poets and pundits write about "Let Me Off Uptown"

and "Hi Ho Trailus Boot Whip" ("Hip and unhappy," the lyric went) and all that crazy,

scattish stuff you laid down in studios,

they may not know what to make of you. That's quite okay.

You loved and survived the jazz life, whose sound you audibly loved.

Joe Morello, while Dave Brubeck sometimes kicked up chords like thunderous hoofbeats, you,

the childhood violinist turned drummer, made the ground he galloped on dependable ground;

supple enough to give, and solid enough to give and take.

Gene Wright, what was a hard-plucking bassist like you doing up there

in back of Brubeck and Paul Desmond?

Ooo, and pushing the band so effortlessly!

Uphill, downhill—from take zero to "Take Five" storming heaven on tiptoe,

and through a side entrance.

Joe Morello

b. 1928

First of all, a fantastic technician. Joe could play any meter you wanted him to play. I think Joe was tamed by Gene Wright, whose nickname was "the Senator." I only know this: when they were stationed at the Blackhawk, when they were the house band, Eugene convinced Joe, "We need to get the basic sound." And so Joe would kind of pull himself in except when he was soloing. The stuff with Dave Brubeck is exciting because Brubeck was percussive and when they made these discoveries about those different meters—Middle East rhythms and so forth—Joe Morello was the perfect drummer. Philly Joe [Jones] couldn't have done it. He might've done some of the meters, but so far as a tympanic approach—Joe Morello's was a tympanic approach.

Eugene Wright

b. 1923

Eugene and Joe together, they made a difference in whether or not the Brubeck Quartet had any swing feeling. And Eugene had a lot to do with that, man. He had an awful lot to do with that.

35

Mary Lou Willia

1910–1981

Reacher for whole suns,
full moons, half notes,
quarter notes, rests,
you brought back grand
respect, forever up to date.
Player, composer, arranger,
and key consultant to
Erroll Garner, Bud Powell,
Thelonious Monk, Marian
McPartland, and mother
to how many others, you
start with heart. You touch
as much. You suffered
enough to repair to Paris,
convert to Catholicism.
Spirit churned in you. You
made your most sublime
offering to the world: your
brilliance, your beauty.

I knew of her stature and respected her stature, so I had to do an elbow on a couple of white photographers. She was on the stage; she had on a girdle. When you were down low, you could look up her dress. I made my position was off to the side a little bit. From where we were, because elevation, you looked under the piano. These guys started hunching one They wanted to take pictures of that. Every time the guy next to me ra camera, I'd bump him. I did this about three times. They got the message.

I had quite a few of her recordings then, especially the Mass she did for St. de Porres. My feeling about her was kind of a worship thing, even though ther pieces of hers that didn't feel as if they had a swing to them. In spite of the st meter, not *tempo*, but *meter*, I could tell the music was there. She had a serious breakdown. I had one of her business cards, a miniature card, about twice the a postage stamp. I gave it away in one of my weak moments, when I should've I saw her as an idol. No question about it. I knew I wasn't witnessing her in th milieu. I knew she wouldn't be able to show her stuff at the Monterey Jazz Fes

She reminded me of Ralph Bunche. I shot him once during UN Day at UC Berk Mary Lou reminded me of his dignity. You have to pay attention to her.

"Rabbit," they called you. Was it your ears?

Was it the way your nose quivered above your horn's mouthpiece?

You sniffed out melody. You always had your way with a ballad; you took your time.

You always took your time. Rabbits do not.

38

Johnny Hodges was a master of tone. The greatest day I had with Duke's band was the day when they were having an Ellington seminar at Cal. Two days. It was just an accident. The band was rehearsing at ten or eleven in the morning at Zellerbach Auditorium. I came in the door and I had plenty of film with me. I stayed all day, taking pictures of them. In between I was giving photography lessons to [baritone saxophonist] Harry Carney and [clarinetist] Jimmy Hamilton and the trumpet player [Herbie] Jones. They were all into cameras; they were happy. It was a thrill to pass on technical stuff to them, which they didn't have time to dig out. They were doing one piece and [star tenor saxophonist] Paul Gonsalves was juiced. Duke made him go over the piece over and over again. He would call out the bar numbers: "Now go back to nine," and so forth. The rest of the band, like Johnny Hodges, they would sit with their hands crossed over their horns. They'd been through it a million times. The trombone section, they got up and sat in pew—I mean, the *auditorium* chairs. They had to be some reading asses. I could tell they appreciated the regular pay.

Even when Duke was way out of earshot, you heard no negativism. They went through the rehearsal with just segments. Duke wrote up until the last minute. There was one situation where Billy Strayhorn was sitting next to Duke in the rehearsal hall and Paul played something that made Billy say, "Duke, would you tell Paul that that's a D in bar nine?" Paul answered back, "Naw, that's not what it is here." "Duke, tell him that's what I wrote." Paul held up the music and said, "Show me the D." It was a mistake in copying. Other than a situation like that…It was amazing to me. I thought about how these guys wouldn't bad-mouth Paul either, even though he was slowing up the show. To look down the aisle and to see Hamilton, Gonsalves, Hodges, and then Harry. Whatever you put in front of them, they could play. The music always had some swing to it.

Jimmy Rushing

1903–1972

Aw, you Count Basie sender of telegrams,

always alive and all full of jive and woes and wisdom, too!

Times gettin' tougher than tough, you shouted.

Things gettin' rougher than rough. And Don't the moon look lonesome /

Shinin' through the trees?

And Rinehart, Rinehart, I'm a most indiff'rent guy /

But I love my Vincent baby / And that's no Harvard lie

On the record you made with Dave Brubeck's quartet—

with him backing you and you backing them—

you suddenly uttered: "Play it, Home!" And all y'all did just that.

Shhh, shhh, get outta here, Jimmy! Blues shouter—

that's how they labeled you,

slow to note the hot comfort of your ragged whisper.

You meant every breath of it, didn't you, Mister Five by Five?

Dizzy Gillespie
1917–1993
Billy Eckstine
1914–1993

A real conversational exchange, and the body movements that go with it.
The linguist Kenneth Johnson, whose specialty was
African retentions in black American speech, had taught both me and
Charles about haptics (spatial relationships between speakers).
There's a whole lot happening in these seven shots.
By their movements and faces, you can tell that Dizzy and Billy
(and Budd Johnson as he gets dressed in the background)
are paying close attention to each another.

Budd Johnson was in the background changing his clothes. The interesting thing about a series like that or scenes like that is that I can't listen to the conversation. What I'm fixed on are the body dynamics. Billy had his valve trombone up. Until today there are a lot of people who don't know he played valve trombone, and trumpet before that.

I'm reminded of something I learned from Ken Johnson, the linguist. An Africanism among black males is to be talking to one another, and then make a point, then walk away or even circle around. Dizzy did just that. I wanted to keep taking pictures. It was okay to even show Dizzy blurred because I wanted to show the motion. And then at the end of this exchange—and I couldn't recall it, not even if someone said, "Here's a million dollars"—but at the end Dizzy just picked up his horn and they started doodling. Camaraderie.

I'd shot a similar sequence of Art Blakey and Billy Eckstine at Masonic Auditorium in the dressing room. They were so loose with "MF" and everything else that I know if I had been a white dude, they wouldn't have done that. They knew I was in the room. They also knew I wasn't a writer. They didn't have to worry about being quoted. I actually felt privileged.

Your bands in the Twenties accentuate a century of stuff to watch for
and things to come.

Sweet or hot, from New York and Pops to San Francisco hilltops,

what you played stayed. They nicknamed you Fatha, but you were a Mutha.

Earl Hines

1903–1983

Hines had so much history, and even I knew his history. I was very satisfied being close to him, because I had a little ten-inch Brunswick of him and Louis Armstrong from 1927, and I made myself listen to it fifty years ago, during the bebop thing. Because I knew. These guys started this thing.

Gabor Szabo

1936–1982

With chops tough enough to bust you out of Dodge,
you packed your guitar and fled Budapest right when Russian tanks were rolling into Hungary.
You hit California and bowled jazz over.
Chico Hamilton, Charles Lloyd, Gary McFarland, Lena Horne—
they launched you.
You sailed out into your own bright, calm, rocking, dark sea. A songful bon voyage indeed.

47

"The drummer knows what to do,"
Duke Ellington told you, when you complained that he wrote music
for everybody else in the band but you.
He was right. Why else did he call you "the world's greatest drummer"?
From the very start, you drummed from the heart,
and what we hear runs deeper than skin-deep.

Louie Bellson
b. 1924

They didn't dare call you by your real nickname of Cannibal, so Manhattan vinyl packagers changed it to Cannonba

Still, you ate up everything: ballads, blues, shuffle tunes, the moon.

Late in your fame, a private chef sometimes traveled with the band.

We loved the sound of your horn, the sound of your voice, the sound of you live and direct.

"He spent his childhood running away and ducking Nazis and stuff,"
Cannonball Adderley said of you, Joe Zawinul, introducing us to you at a 1962 concert at Berkeley Auditorium.
No one would've guessed you'd go on to write some of the funkiest, soul-greasing songs for tha
nor that you'd hook up with Wayne Shorter to form Weather Report.
Which one of the Lost Tribes are you descended from?

Julian Cannonball Adderley
1928–1975

Joe Zawinul
1932–2007

It's hard to ignore the charisma. Cannonball was playing like he was talking to people, just like he was talking verbally. You can tell that he was committed to communicating—not just playing the music, but communicating with the listener. It wasn't just the rhythmic soul stuff as such. His brother was the same way. I don't want to say his brother played a little harsher horn; Cannonball was more legato than Nat in his phrasing. It was hard not to listen to Cannonball, because the way he played up and down his horn, it wasn't just showing technique. He was always exciting—the fact that he would *talk* to the audience, you didn't see a lot of musicians talking with audiences. Miles should have let *him* talk when he was in the band.

Two Basses Mating

Is this a kiss? Is this at all like "Two Bass Hit"? Early in the morning, late at night, two trees fell and kept falling in love. Somewhere around the middle of the twentieth century, the Sauter-Finnegan Orchestra recorded "When Two Trees Fall in Love." Of course trees mate. The wood from which Charles Mingus' basses were formed shares a common ancestry: Ours.

53

Bass players just plain love to fiddle and fool with, and finally waylay the cello with delicacy and tact.

Could it be a yin and yang thing?

Could it be that nestled within the lion that roars is a kitten who purrs

and sometimes leaps into trees, and soars?

Ray Brown (with cello)
1926–2002

The gut strings, the wood of the bass. It's touch. Unlike some of the young guys who came after him, Ray was never out to show you how fast he was. Ray Brown's tone and the sound of his instrument—that *was* his touch. I'm curious today about who got his bass, and if anyone could get anywhere close to him. It's just beautiful to hear his grace notes.

You had no trouble blending in with Texas-born Ornette Coleman's avant-garde band. You were from Shenandoah, I⦁

You grew up singing on the radio with your country songster family.

You knew you could always get down and play you some down-home stuff, some folk songs.

You speak right up, you sing right out!

Charlie Haden
b. 1937

A very serious bass player. I like his tone, too. I heard him with David Izenzon, when they were with Ornette Coleman. That didn't particularly excite me. What I really listened to was the album he did with Hank Jones, doing religious tunes. Charlie, without being arrogant—any manifest arrogance, if you will—is a very fine musician. He gives you the impression of being serious about his work. Ornette gave him a lot of license. This is only my opinion. I did spend time listening to them because they were such a challenge. I also think Haden gave some legitimacy to Ornette's stuff that Ornette alone couldn't give. Okay? Charlie now, considering what he's been through…I haven't listened to him much recently. I don't have any stories about him. I didn't get a chance to hang around him. Quite frankly, I wish I had. He seems like he has a lot of class to him, the way he presents himself as a musician—a lot of dignity. He was hardly ever a clown.

"And David danced before the Lord with all his might," sayeth Samuel in the King James version.

"And David was girded with a linen ephod."

A linen what? Well, Mr. Briggs, that suit of celebration looks linen enough,

and surely worshipful enough to dance with joy before anything holy,

which shakes and rolls right out and comes right down to every living,

watchful, listening presence.

Bunny Briggs
b. 1923

Now, taking a still of a dancer, if I'm shooting with available light—and to this day I never want to interrupt or insult a scene with flash—the first thing I do is study and observe. Does he have some pattern to when he stops, when he's actually frozen? Then I have to anticipate this. The other thing I want to do is show the emotion. So in this sequence I shot of him, I intentionally wanted one of the last frames to be blurred, actively showing motion.

From royalty, yes, you hail from this.

With hang-back timing and a tone

as princely and majestic superb as the sound

your brother Ernie Royal conjured from a trumpet,

you, holding forth on alto saxophone and clarinet,

lit up our nights.

Did your ears

and fingers

recall your beginnings

as a violinist and

guitarist?

Marshall Royal

1912–1995

60

Rooted in the blue-black soil of her Carolina girlhood, she was the diva.

She could purr and roar; she could dive and soar—and more.

You didn't play with Nina, not unless you could go her distance—

and what delicious, twisting distances they are.

If you couldn't run with the sun, send sound underground

or swim her troubled waters, you couldn't play with Nina Simone.

You might get hurt.

Nina Simone

1933–2003

Oh, man! Nina. She was an icon. The commitment she made to music is so obvious. First of all, it's not hard to listen to her. She was relatively easy to take pictures of. The dynamics of her playing—I mean, sometimes it's show time—but the dynamics of her playing provided the norm. She's one of the few people whose music I can't un-listen to while I'm taking pictures. The music lets me know where her peaks are. Shooting in available light without flash, you've got to learn the artist's moves real quick if you haven't seen them before. With Nina, it was very unpredictable, very unpredictable. From the standpoint of her body movements, you really had to be tight; you had to anticipate. Her body movements were easier to shoot with a range-finder camera than with a single-lens reflex because the only thing moving in a range-finder camera is the shutter. If I take up the slack in the shutter-release button, I never lose her image. That's because I never get a blacked-out screen like I do on a single-lens reflex, which never lets you see the image you actually took. With a range-finder, you never lose the image; you can get that little peak you might've been looking for, the one she might've been doing for that particular song. That's the graphic part of it. I always heard her music when I was taking pictures.

Dizzy Gillespie
1917–1993

At Club Paradise, in the 1940s, you hit on my mother, or so she says.
At the Jazz Workshop, San Francisco, in the 1960s, you hit on my wife. If she and I had given birth to a
daughter rather than a son, you would've hit on her, too, had you lived. Like countless others, I was a hopelessly add
admirer. From swing and "Rhythm-a-ning" to blue-bop and Cu-bop, you knew what you blew.
You cared enough to see that we all got it, too. I miss your laugh.

Connie Kay
1927–1994

Never before had I met such a splendidly gifted and world-weary foursome as you,
John Lewis, Milt Jackson, and Percy Heath.
It was in California at Paul Masson Vineyards, at a dinner before your performance.
On stage that night, you celebrated.
As you pumped and re-circulated life-blood to the band, you made everything sound
and feel like the first breath I'd ever drawn. Inhale, exhale—just like that.

I loved Connie Kay keeping time. Connie Kay had little things he would do in 4/4 time that enhanced the time. Let me tell you. The dream was set in Baltimore. I was walking down this main street and, on an adjacent parallel street, I heard this cymbal beat. (Connie Kay had a cymbal beat that he enhanced.) I heard it coming. It was an eighteenth-century vintage scene. You know how fire trucks had a guy who rang a bell? This was a horse-drawn fire truck that Connie Kay was sitting up on with his drums, man, and was keeping the time. That was the bell, the fire bell. It woke me up. Man, I woke up laughing. I said, "That beat is so in my head!" Connie Kay has a lot of variety on his ride cymbal. He was perfect. I'm walking down the street in this dream, and it was an alley, a really narrow alley, so narrow only one vehicle could go down it; unduly narrow, more narrow than it was in the real world. I stood there because I heard him on this other street. I waited at that street to see him go by, because I couldn't believe, in the dream, that I was having the dream of Connie Kay taking that ride-cymbal beat. I didn't go back to sleep. I just kept laughing.

Milt Jackson

1923–1999

Dizzy once said that as long as the MJQ had you, Milt Jackson, everything would be valid and jazz-okay.

You, Milt, with your heartbreaking ballads and shattering blues.

Not knowing you would soon take leave, it was my pleasure to treat you to lunch.

The occasion: an Ellington centennial guitarist our fellow Detroiter Kenny Burrell had produced at

UCLA. You told me sad and joyful stories.

I went back up to my room and laughed and cried. Milt, you melt it all down.

Any tune you can name, Milt could play. Once you know the lyrics to a song, you can hear Milt doing them. It still amazes me to this day what he can get out of a vibraharp. The other thing that Milt introduced was softer mallets, softer than Lionel Hampton's.

The one thing I've always held against John Lewis was his soloing over and on top of Milt Jackson. You have to listen through the piano—on the Atlantic sessions anyway—to hear Milt. Sometimes I think Milt was just playing for himself.

Milt was a full composer. If he finished up a chorus with a phrase, you could hear him pick up where he left off.

Paul Desmond

1924–1977

You changed your name. You thought Breitenfeld sounded too Irish, so Desmond became your moniker.

Your favorite singer, Billie Holiday, was born Eleanora Fagan Gough.

Literary-drawn, you wrote short stories you never published.

You published many a short story, with erudite quotations and all, on your exquisite saxophone.

O these self-invented Americans!

Elvin Jones

1927–2004

When cool came up, it didn't mean you.

Lean and fierce, a hard rain falling on roof-
tops and trees, you timed and seasoned;

you showered voices and melody with
song-like rushes of sound.

You played hard, Elvin. You played for keeps.

Energy. Who was he with at Monterey? Oh, he was with the Gil Evans band. A lot of energy. For a guy of his stature—and I'm just talking about non-playing for one quick second—he wouldn't hesitate to let you know how strong he was. He reminded me of a guy I grew up with. He had long, thin muscles that were strong. He reminded me of Rod Carew, the baseball player. He reminded me of Preacher Roe, the pitcher. Oh, I was visualizing all the thin athletes who demonstrated strength. In fact, what he did at one of the rehearsals: some guy said something to him and Elvin just reached over and picked him up off the floor. This was in the barn, the rehearsal barn. He said something (I don't know what it was); he didn't curse him out or anything… But energy-wise—man!

Soviet Premier Yuri Andropov declared you the greatest trumpeter of the twentieth century. Listening to everybody's Miles story, you'd never know how you and glory hooked up. Epoch upon epoch, you connected. You, the Juilliard class-cutter, Big Apple bebopper out of East St. Louis, Birth of the Cool, Kind of Blue, Sketches of Spain, Nefertiti, Someday My Prince Will Come, In a Silent Way, Miles Smiles, Bitches Brew—all of it with you at the center, reinventing the trumpet and music alike.

First of all, Miles, when I asked him to do some pictures—this was at the Both/And Club in San Francisco—the second word out of his mouth was "You must be outta your MF'ing mind." He had posed with photographer Jim Marshall in the gym and everything. It took all my nerve to approach him. I knew about his crustiness. I just let it go.

What I was a witness to was his metamorphosis, if you will. The first time at Monterey, he was in his continentals; he set the stage for that. The Ivy League thing, you know, with three buttons and natural shoulders—and of course I was able to know what it was all about because I had worked in a men's clothing store. The next year I saw him in a continental thing. The jacket was cut away, the pants were narrow and well off the shoes. Then the next year he'd morphed into wearing the big glasses and a leather jacket with strings hanging down off of it. And the next year was all these colors. So he was trying to morph into the rock thing. And he did.

As a performer—Miles' music was always beautiful. I was at the Blackhawk when they did the *Friday Night/Saturday Night* album. I stayed around Friday night until the club closed at two a.m. Saturday. Then I went next door to listen to the playback of the tapes engineer Wally Heider had made. The music was fantastic...to hear it again.

BILLY

Billy Eckstine

1914–1993

What a lot of people don't know is that B. was an instrumentalist too. He played trumpet and valve trombone. You could hear this in his voice, the way he phrased. We're talking about presentation—and dignity.

Matinee idol to my mother's 1940s and 1950s generation, your deep baritone voice traveled;

it seeped way down inside us. According to *Ebony* (or was it *Jet*?),

Princess Margaret was one of your persistent fans.

Women wore your glow; young guys like me wore your Mister B. shirts with their broad, arching collars

73

Carmen McRae

1922–1994

Cleopatric in profile, you sang like a soul who went way, way back. The feelings you breathed into them validated even the most standard of ballads. And you could jump-tune, too. To "Straight No Chaser" you delivered Sally Swisher's lyric: "Well, Monk said it straight, / 'It's out of town when you wait.'" In your savvy voice, the piano you used to play sounds still.

I could see the layout when I took it. I could see the print. As a young person, Carmen had a magnificent profile. It was Egyptian. Before I even took that picture, I kept seeing that profile. She was a different person in profile than she was straight on. I also wanted to isolate her in the frame so there was nothing else for you to look at, which is why I had that background black. The first prints that I made of this were portrait layout. I said, "That doesn't even show enough black." So I printed it in landscape, which gave me more black space, black space. And I had to be sure that the print showed black as opposed to gray. I always saw her as a beautiful woman.

One of my very first photographs—when I started concentrating on jazz photography—was of Carmen playing an upright piano and singing in the original Longshoreman's Hall on Golden Gate Avenue, San Francisco. The upright piano was against the wall, but I took pictures of her anyway. She was one of my first subjects.

McRae

Muddy Waters
(McKinley Morganfield)
1915–1983

He got a black cat bone. He got a mojo, too.

He got the John the Conquerer root. He gon' mess with you.

That's the electrifying Delta-cum-Chicago Muddy Waters we think we know.

There was another: the Muddy who only drank Mumm's Champagne, owned real estate, handed out

money to his hard-luck buddies, and jammed with

Dizzy Gillespie at Smitty's Corner on Chicago's South Side. Is this poetry enough, or what?

Jimmy Rushing
1903–1972

Mister Five by Five, straight up and down, you shouted the blues.

You shouted 'em out. Songs sounded like you'd personally tried out all the stuff the words maintained

before you sprang it on listeners and dancers.

That was pretty much the way you tested out the story you worked, wasn't it? But you come from a

whole family of Kansas City musicians and entertainers.

Who wouldn't give anything to know what you and Muddy Waters were talking about?

I didn't get to hear that conversation, but I also saw Jimmy Rushing more than I did Muddy Waters, even though I appreciated Muddy as a blues singer. I've got a lot of Jimmy Rushing: the early Columbia stuff with Basie. Rushing I appreciated the same way I appreciated Dinah Washington and Joe Williams. Uniquely—because of their diction. They were blues singers. Their diction was perfect. It was the ultimate in urban blues. You could also tell Jimmy was a musician. Now I have a DVD of him playing piano on one of Ralph J. Gleason's *Jazz Casual* TV things. With him, you can feel the beat. He could sing behind the beat, catch up. You could feel the swing in his voice. I've got some good shots of him on stage. Too many of my shots are on stage. I wish I had more shots like this.

I felt really deficient with Muddy Waters because I hadn't listened. I'd *read* a lot about country blues and urban blues. I knew he had status—and that's an understatement—and, because I didn't know it well enough, I'm sure I paid more attention to his music than to bebop music. Muddy, documented, to me was a source of blues and jazz. Even with amplification, it was still legitimate. I never looked down on country blues singers. I mean, there were guys in my neighborhood—it was urban—and they'd be sitting on the steps with a guitar.

John Lewis
1920–2001

Franco Ambrosetti
b. 1941

With fingers in motion, the same fingers with which you mastered the keys of trumpet and flugelhorn,
you're making some powerful point.
The controlled smile on Monterey Jazz Festival music director John Lewis' face says:
"Yes, I hear you, *but...*" Some ifs and ands doubtless flowered in the music you made that night.

He and John were having some kind of argument, or discussion—a softer way of saying it, I guess. I made John second. Right? Musically, John was a beautiful single-note player. He had swing to his stuff. He didn't flood you with his left hand; it wasn't too busy. It was intermittent enough that it was easy to follow what he was doing. Very, very melodic—no getting around that part. Clearly his charts were Bachian, no getting around that part. I got turned on to Bach, man, through the Brandenburgs. And the fifth one—that's all open, or mostly open—turned me on the most. I tell people, here's the history of jazz: Bach, Gottschalk, and then late nineteenth-century, with what we call jazz coming in. Control—that's what I captured in these shots of John Lewis. As a musician he was outstandingly simple, and the fact that he sang with it made it for sure legitimate. Not as much as Bud Powell, of course.

Are you the same Big Black who lived on Potrero Hill, hung out in North Beach,
and held down a gig as a cook in South San Francisco?
Pianist Randy Weston, Africa-oriented, loved what you did to a drum with your hands.
You did up everything just as big as you kept up your cheer-driven spirit.

Big Black (Daniel Ray)
b. 1934

"Black had more than his usual accumulation of drums set on one side of the room. Tumbas, congas, bongos, miscellaneous percussion devices. Black... was wearing a coarse-thread African shirt that hung over his pants. His hands aren't just large, they're astonishingly muscular. They seem to have joints that the rest of us don't possess, muscles that are unseen by non-finger-drummers."

—*Philip Elwood*
in his liner notes for the 1982 *African Fusion* (Big Black and Anthony Wheaton)

81

Charles "Cootie" William

1910–1985

"What can you say about a guy whose nickname was Cootie?"
jazz impresario Orrin Keepnews once asked.
Well, you infected not only our dancing bodies, but our ecstasy-driven psyches as well.
The grooves you laid, the high hellos, your brassy sighed inflections of yearning and hope.
You scaled the heights, you plunged and plumbed the depths of us.

Jimmy Hamilton

1917–1994

Sophisticated Ellingtonian from head to toe, you seemed to know which notes to float and which ones to squirrel away for some other day.
Always up to something good, you sounded calm and collected,
yet you were anything but cool.

Don Ellis

1934–1978

Don Ellis got into the 5/4, the 7/4, the tricky 9/8 signatures of time as sound.
At this, Ellis and his bands excelled. It's as if he never missed a chance to beat the odds.
Trumpet the news: Time colors blues.

As the great crowd pleaser and heart teaser Illinois Jacquet consorts with John Lewis (bebop minimalist and Bach baroque fuguist), Niels-Henning Örsted Pedersen, the Great Dane of bassists, leans in to listen, and then sits in. We know that Jacquet's wife takes care of his hair, but who picked out this elegant plaid suit for Lewis? As for Pedersen, he always wore nothing dressier than a smile, and his heart on the sleeve of his bass case.

Illinois Jacquet
1922–2004

John Lewis
1920–2001

The picture that you're seeing—I'm so proud of it—is sharp. Illinois gave me a feeling of cleanness. I don't know if he ever was a druggie. This picture doesn't have that high, tacky gloss to it. It's a swing moment. Illinois Jacquet was a fine musician. I'm really glad I got to hear him later on, as opposed to what we heard from him as a kid, when he was doing all that honking with the Lionel Hampton band. We called him Fulla-Noise Jacquet. First time I saw and heard Illinois Jacquet was with Lionel Hampton, "Flying Home," sat through three or four stage shows. They were running up and down the aisle. About the third show you'd have this headache. But the headache wasn't from the stage show; the headache is from the movie. You had to sit through the movie, too. Later on I discovered what a very fine balladeer he was. He played bass clarinet, too.

87

When Duke Ellington sent for you to sing in his first sacred concert at Grace Cathedral,
San Francisco, you were Esther Morrow. Now you're Queen Esther *Marrow,* one of gospel's crown jewels.
In your bones the spirit still moves as powerfully as when your voice graced us in the beginning.

Esther Morrow

c. 1943

She had such a big and powerful voice; it startled me at first. When I think about how I sat next to Billy Strayhorn and Duke, who were rehearsing the band…and I'm sitting right there, man. When it comes to photographs, Duke is a hog-hound anyway. One time on the stage I saw him elbow Esther Morrow out of the way. She was singing. Duke was actually following me. I was moving from side to side. I didn't believe it at first. He looked over, and I ducked him, then he found me. I said, "Well, I be damned!" And then he found me. That was all right, but I just didn't believe it was happening.

Glimpsing the funny-looking two of you at mid-twentieth century, Miles and you, walking mid-Manhattan sidewalks—
a short black man and a tall redheaded Irish American—who could have known you would be giving birth?
And *Birth of the Cool*, a landmark album, the world still plays and plunders.
Tell me, how did you, a New York boy, get to invent West Coast jazz?

Gerry Mulligan

1927–1996

Ernie Andrews

b. 1927

Sing your heart out, Ernie Andrews! Like, what else have you been up to for decades and decades? Johnny Hartman warned about letting critics and reviewers pin the "singer's singer" on superb artists. But they pulled that stuff on you. You got back, though. You lived to let your greatness grow even grander. Go easy on us, Ernie. More, more!

Ray Nance

1913–1976

With your middle name of Willis—as in where there's a will, there are ways—you started out on piano, took up violin, taught yourself trumpet and even tap-danced and sang more than a taste. Your generous appetite for elegance and perfection laid the table and kept wine flowing in banquet proportions at the Ellington feasts. Hey, Ray, what you say!

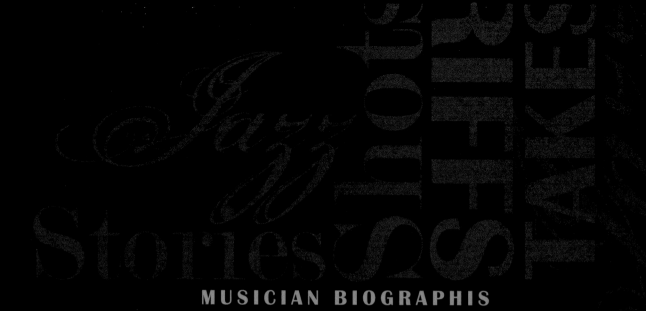

MUSICIAN BIOGRAPHIS

Julian Cannonball Adderley
(1928-1975)

When in the 1950s he gave up his high school band director gig in Florida to come up to New York, alto saxophonist Julian Adderley hit the jazz scene hard. Right away fans recognized him as a giant in the tradition of Charlie Parker, but Adderley played with a joyfulness and zest that seemed to be as large as his appetite for good cooking. Cannonball became a polite euphemism for "Cannibal," his original nickname. Combining the gospel-tinged, funk trends that were leaking into jazz from vernacular black music, Adderley, working with his younger cornet-playing brother, Nat, and pianist Bobby Timmons, hit it big. Genial and eloquent, Adderley wowed live audiences. Recordings Adderley made with the Miles Davis Quintet that also featured John Coltrane and Bill Evans ensure their permanent stature in jazz heaven.
• Somethin' Else *(Blue Note)*
• Greatest Hits *(EMI)*

Franco Ambrosetti
(b. 1941)

The son of famed Swiss saxophonist Flavio Ambrosetti, Franco Ambrosetti was trained as a pianist but taught himself to play trumpet and flugelhorn. A cofounder of pianist George Gruntz's Concert Jazz Band, he leans towards late and post-bop stylings. One of Europe's best-known players, Ambrosetti works often in the U.S. and has performed with Kenny Barron, Joe Henderson, Dexter Gordon, Michael Brecker, and Phil Woods.
• Live at the Blue Note *with Seamus Blake, Kenny Barron, Ira Coleman, Victor Lewis (Enja)*

Ernie Andrews
(b. 1927)

"Ernie Andrews has managed to be both popular and underrated throughout his lengthy career," says critic Scott Yanow of this exuberant, evergreen, gospel-rooted jazz singer. *Big City* may be his best-known album, recorded with Cannonball Adderley in 1967. Recording and performing since his teens (he was discovered by songwriter Joe Greene in 1947), Andrews has worked with Benny Carter and Gerald Wiggins. He traveled throughout North and South America for a decade with the Harry James Band.
• This Is Ernie Andrews *(Verve)*

Louis Bellson
(b. 1924)

Born with the florid Italian name of Luigi Paulino Alfredo Francesco Antonio Balassoni, Louie Bellson is no joke. When Duke Ellington called him the world's greatest drummer, the master meant it. A teenage phenomenon, his playing powered the big bands of Benny Goodman, Tommy Dorsey, and Harry James. His marriage in 1952 to singer-comedienne Pearl Bailey caused a sensation. For Duke's band, Bellson composed "Skin Deep" and "The Hawk Talks," two memorable and lasting vehicles on which his playing was featured. Whether as soloist or timekeeper, Bellson's drumming—crisply musical, tasteful, and inventive—crackles with feeling.
• *Duke Ellington,* Ellington Uptown *(Columbia Legacy)*

Big Black
(b. 1934)

Daniel Ray is the "real name" of this dynamic percussionist whose passion is the conga drum. Stunned by the power and beauty of Afro-Cuban music, he took up conga drumming as a teenager. Journeys to Florida and the Bahamas led to his joining Lord Flea's calypso band and later the Calypso Eddy Trio. It was during his frequent performances with pianists Ray Bryant and Randy Weston that he attracted public attention in the 1960s. Big Black played, too, with Eric Dolphy, Junior Cook, and Dizzy Gillespie, who all loved this master conguero's rhythmic elasticity and deeply sensitive touch.
• *Randy Weston,* Berkshire Blues *(Black Lion)*

Bunny Briggs
(b. 1923)

In 1989 Bunny Briggs was nominated for Broadway's Tony Award as Best Actor for his tap-dancing role as Hoofer in *Black and Blue*. He is "the dancer's dancer" who Duke Ellington singled out to feature in the role of David, who danced before the Lord, in Ellington's first Sacred Concert, performed at San Francisco's Grace Cathedral. Briggs, whose career began in vaudeville when he was five, appeared on Ed Sullivan's *Toast of the Town* irregularly. Watching him dance is like watching the spirit of jazz itself take wing.
• No Maps on My Taps—*1979 film stars Bunny Briggs, Sandman Sims, Chuck Green, Lionel Hampton (Direct Cinema Ltd.)*

Ray Brown
(1926–2002)

Ray Brown, one of jazz's all-time great bassists, was once married to Ella Fitzgerald, another of jazz's all-time greats. From the 1940s through the early twenty-first century, he set the standard for precision and emotional eloquence. His first New York gig was with Dizzy Gillespie. He toured with producer Norman Granz's *Jazz at the Philharmonic,* became the first bassist back when Milt Jackson led the Modern Jazz Quartet, before John Lewis took over, then played and toured the world for fifteen years with the Oscar Peterson Trio. In his later years, Brown became a formidable jazz cellist. He has left the world hundreds of outstanding performances on record.
• *Bud Powell,* Blues in the Closet *(Verve)*
• The Oscar Peterson Trio at the Stratford Shakespearian Festival *(Polygram)*

Miles Davis
(1926–1991)

Miles Davis once stated that the history of jazz could be summed up in four words: "Louis Armstrong" and "Charlie Parker." Davis, whose playing reflects his musicianly scholarship (Miles modernizes many of Armstrong's classic licks), brought a new and enduring sound to jazz. All over the world, trumpeters imitate his muted, songlike style. But Miles Davis was a bandleading innovator, too. While still a teenager enrolled at Juilliard, he met and played with Charlie Parker. By 1949, with the recording of the album *Birth of the*

Cool, he was stepping out of the bebop cradle into new musical territory. Davis would continue through ensuing decades to set the pace for jazz's rejuvenation and renewal. His orchestral collaborations with arranger/composer Gil Evans, his small group performances with John Coltrane, Cannonball Adderley, Bill Evans, and later with Herbie Hancock, Wayne Shorter, Ron Carter, John McLaughlin, Chick Corea, and drummer Tony Williams—all four decades of his brilliant career continue to shape the landscape of jazz.

• The Legendary Prestige Quintet Sessions *(Prestige/Fantasy/Milestone)*
• Kind of Blue *(Sony)*
• Sketches of Spain *(Sony)*
• Live in Zurich *with John Coltrane, Wynton Kelly, Paul Chambers, Jimmy Cobb (Gambit)*
• Live at the 1963 Monterey Jazz Festival *(Monterey Jazz Festival boxed set)*

Paul Desmond
(1924–1977)

Paul Emil Breitenfeld was his given name, but he didn't like it. Desmond, a closet fiction writer, once said that he wanted to get from his alto saxophone a sound like a dry martini. Lester Young, the tenor saxophonist and pioneer developer of the so-called cool style, deeply influenced Desmond. From the time they met in San Francisco in the late 1940s, Desmond and Dave Brubeck hit it off musically. To Brubeck's sometimes heavily chorded piano, Desmond soared up beyond clouds into blue skies. During the sixteen years he spent with the Dave Brubeck Quartet (1951–1967), Desmond established a reputation as an elegant, original musical stylist. With their 1959 recording of "Take Five," the group hit the jackpot. Desmond's composition in ancient 5/4 time became jazz's first million-seller.

• Easy Living *(RCA)*
• The Dave Brubeck Quartet at Carnegie Hall *(Sony)*

Billy Eckstine
(1914–1993)

William Clarence Eckstine was his birth name. Eckstine, who played trumpet and valve trombone, formed and led the first bop big band in the 1940s. Not surprisingly, his band roster included Charlie Parker, Dizzy Gillespie, Dexter Gordon, Budd Johnson, and pianist-vocalist Sarah Vaughan. At a time when bobby-soxed teenage girls were swooning to Frank Sinatra, Billy Eckstine—with his deep, smooth baritone voice—became the first black male singer to make the hit parade time and time again. His suave, matinee idol looks didn't hurt.

• Everything I Have Is Yours: The Best of the MGM Years *(MGM, 2-CD set)*
• The Swinging Mr. B and His Orchestra *with Sarah Vaughan (Original Jazz Classics)*

Duke Ellington
(1899–1974)

A consummate pianist, composer, arranger, innovator and showman, Edward Kennedy "Duke" Ellington was the most prolific of American composers. Citing the orchestra as his instrument, he often wrote specifically for one or another of his illustrious band members: trumpeters Bubber Miley, Rex Stewart, and Cootie Williams, saxophonists Johnny Hodges, Ben Webster, Harry Carney, and Paul Gonsalves. According to pianist Earl Hines, "Duke showed the world that jazz could do something besides straight-ahead swing." Ellington tapped into European classical forms and explored the tonalities of Asian and African musical traditions, and he expressed his social and political concerns in such pieces as the suites *Black, Brown and Beige* and *A Tone Parallel to Harlem.* "Take the 'A' Train," his theme song, was penned by Billy Strayhorn, with whom Ellington closely collaborated for decades.

• Masterpieces by Ellington *(Sony)*
• Ellington at Newport 1956 *(Sony)*
• Money Jungle *with Charles Mingus and Max Roach (Blue Note)*

Don Ellis
(1934–1978)

Right after he graduated from Boston University, Los Angeles–born trumpeter and flugelhornist Don Ellis (born Donald Johnson Ellis) started playing in the big bands of Charlie Barnet, Ray McKinley and Maynard Ferguson. By the early 1960s, he had become a dedicated experimenter. He was in sympathetic company when he played with George Russell and Eric Dolphy, later recording with Charles Mingus. Influenced by East Asian and South Asian as well as avant-garde European and American music in the classical tradition, he hit the ground running in 1965 with a band that put his name on the jazz map. Unorthodox

99

arrangements and instrumentation (French horn, tuba, two drummers, three bassists) and quirky time signatures (7/8, 9/8, 15/16) characterized the orchestras Ellis led. Moreover, the tireless musician invented a four-valve trumpet and a slide/valve trombone he called the "superbone."
• Live in 3 2/3 4 Time *(Pacific Jazz)*

Dizzy Gillespie
(1917–1993)

Born John Birks Gillespie in Cheraw, South Carolina, he earned the nickname Dizzy from his on-stage clownish behavior. A sideman in the popular black bands of Teddy Hill and Cab Calloway during the 1930s, he had big ears that pushed him to experiment. His own big bands of the 1940s boiled over with the bebop style that he (with Charlie Parker, Thelonious Monk, and others) had co-created. More than anyone else, it was Dizzy Gillespie who brought Afro-Cuban and African rhythms and African colorations to modern American jazz. If ever there was a jazz ambassador, it was Gillespie, whose music is revered on every continent.
• *Dizzy Gillespie, Charlie Christian, Thelonious Monk,* After Hours *(Original Jazz Classics)*
• *Charlie Parker, Dizzy Gillespie, Bud Powell, Charles Mingus, Max Roach,* The Greatest Jazz Concert Ever/Jazz at Massey Hall *(Fantasy)*
• Dizzy Gillespie Sextet *(Pablo Live)*
• Billy Eckstine at Newport in New York 1972 *(Cobblestone)*
• Gillespiana *(Verve)*

Charlie Haden
(b. 1937)

When he was a little boy, broadcasting from his hometown of Shenandoah, Iowa, Charlie Haden sang on a country-western radio program with his mother and father. These folk roots still stick in his music. Jazz listeners became aware of him as the bassist with Ornette Coleman's sensational quartet of the late 1950s. In recent years, Haden has been the leader of Quartet West, a brilliant ensemble whose every performance and recording delivers something fresh. Politically outspoken, Haden has expressed his social views as leader of the Liberation Music Orchestra.
• *Charlie Haden Quartet West,* Haunted Heart *(Polygram)*

Jimmy Hamilton
(1917–1994)

Known mostly for the dry, affecting eloquence of his clarinet work that distinguished him during the quarter-century he played with the Duke Ellington Orchestra (1943–1968), Jimmy Hamilton also played tenor saxophone. His relatively cool approach to clarinet fell away when he played saxophone, which somehow let him get rhythm and blues-ish, even downright raucous, enough to play his heart right out onto his sleeve. With Hamilton's deft, vibrato-less clarinet voice in mind, Ellington composed and recorded such pieces as "Air Conditioned Jungle" and "Ad Lib on Nippon." Hamilton eventually settled in the Virgin Islands, where he became a public school music educator.
• Can't Help Swinging (Prestige)

Earl Hines
(1903–1983)

By the 1920s, Earl "Fatha" Hines had established himself in Chicago as a superbly modern pianist. Hines translated to piano a lot of Louis Armstrong's trumpet ideas. His piano phrasing was hornlike. Bop pianist Bud Powell would later do the same thing with saxophonist Charlie Parker's ideas. With Armstrong, Hines made classic recordings during the Prohibition Era. Hines' dazzling swing bands of the late 1920s actually anticipate bebop. Ever the visionary virtuoso, Hines made San Francisco his home.
• Louis Armstrong, vol. 4, with Earl Hines (Columbia /Legacy)
• Earl Fatha Hines: The Early Years: 1923–1942 (Storyville)

Johnny Hodges
(1906–1970)

For generations of jazz devotees, the sound that Johnny Hodges emitted on alto saxophone was nothing short of sublime. Most fans would settle for beautiful. Balladeer par excellence, Hodges, whose nickname was Rabbit, could hippity-hop and romp and stomp with the rawest of blues swingers. Although he left the Ellington orchestra for several years to form his own small band, he eventually found his way back. To complete the palette from which he painted his orchestral music, Ellington counted on Hodges' sculptable spirit and presence.

101

- *Duke Ellington and Johnny Hodges,* Play the Blues Back to Back *(Verve)*
- *Duke Ellington and Johnny Hodges,* Side By Side *(Verve)*

Milt Jackson
(1923–1999)

Milt Jackson, Detroit born and bred, picked up the vibraphone traditions laid down by Lionel Hampton and Red Norvo and carried them to new levels of power and lyricism. Thoroughly blues-rooted, Bags (some say the nickname came from his sleepy-eyed look) played to the gut as well as the heart. When critics accused the Modern Jazz Quartet of being "conservatory" stodgy, Dizzy Gillespie asserted that as long as Milt Jackson was there, the group would always have soul. When the internationally renowned MJQ broke up for seven years in the 1970s, Bags told *Down Beat* magazine that MJQ now stood for "Milt Jackson Quit."
- *Milt Jackson, Cedar Walton, Ray Brown, Mickey Roker,* It Don't Mean a Thing If You Can't Tap Your Foot to It *(Original Jazz Classics)*

Illinois Jacquet
(1922–2004)

Louisiana-born Jean-Baptiste Illinois Jacquet invented the rowdy rhythm and blues tenor sax sound. He also played Charlie Parker–style alto saxophone, bass clarinet, and easy-listening bassoon. Working sax players of the 1940s and 50s memorized and could recite on demand the teasing, growling solo Jacquet builds up and lays down on Lionel Hampton's 1942 recording of "Flying Home." At live shows, whole audiences would sing along with it as he blew. Jacquet, a superb balladeer, survived his pop hit success, forming his own bands, small and big. By the 1980s he was internationally treasured as a musician.
- The Illinois Jacquet Story *(Proper Records, 4-CD set)*

Elvin Jones
(1927–2004)

The baby brother in a musical family that includes trumpeter Thad Jones and pianist Hank Jones, drummer Elvin Jones was a powerhouse. His fiery, high-intensity playing powered the John Coltrane Quartet during the whole half-decade of its existence

(1960–1965). Prior to his legendary stint with Coltrane, Jones had been a mainstay on Detroit's jazz scene, playing with Yusef Lateef, Barry Harris, Pepper Adams, Donald Byrd, Charles McPherson. Moving to New York in 1955, he worked with Miles Davis, J. J. Johnson, Bud Powell, and Sonny Rollins. The Elvin Jones Jazz Machine is the band he formed and traveled and recorded with during the last decade of his life.
• The Individualism of Gil Evans *(Verve)*

Connie Kay
(1927–1994)

After drummer Kenny Clarke left the Modern Jazz Quartet in the early 1950s, Connie Kay took over and stayed with the illustrious, hard-swinging chamber group for almost forty years. So identified with the MJQ is this great percussionist—whose tasteful, restrained intensity fueled his fellow players—that people forget the other notables with whom Kay performed. They include Stan Getz, Benny Goodman, Coleman Hawkins, Lester Young, Chet Baker, Cannonball Adderley, Tommy Flanagan, and Paul Desmond.
• *Modern Jazz Quartet*, Topsy: This One's for Basie *(Concord Music Group/Pablo)*

John Lewis
(1920–2001)

John Lewis' sparse and spacious piano style epitomizes the minimalist approach to jazz improvisation of which Count Basie is master. Lewis' Army buddies while he was stationed in England during World War II included Milt Jackson and Kenny Clarke. On completing his military service, the New Mexico–born pianist relocated to New York, where, with Clarke's help, he became pianist for the first of Dizzy Gillespie's historic big bop bands. By 1949 Lewis, like Miles Davis, was looking in new directions. He worked with Davis and with saxophonists Gerry Mulligan and Lee Konitz on the legendary *Birth of the Cool* album. His fixation with bop, blues, and baroque music, the music of Sebastian Bach especially, led to the formation of the Modern Jazz Quartet, which for close to fifty years remained an institution unto itself.
• 2 Degrees East, 3 Degrees West *(RCA)*
• *Modern Jazz Quartet*, European Concert *(Label M)*

Esther Marrow: See Esther Morrow

Carmen McRae
(1922–1994)

Carmen McRae is renowned as one of jazz's leading, pace-setting vocalists, but she began as a pianist. She was the intermission pianist at fabled Minton's Playhouse in New York, where bebop is said to have been born. She was married then to drummer legend Kenny Clarke. Ten years before she made her first recordings as a singer, McRae sang briefly with the big bands of Benny Carter, Count Basie, and Mercer Ellington. In the 1950s her singing career took off, and the earthy, urbane performer—admired for her impeccable articulation and all-around musicality—never looked back.
• *Carmen McRae with Mat Mathews,* Easy to Love *(Bethlehem)*
• Carmen Sings Monk *(RCA)*

Charles Mingus
(1922–1979)

Before leading and composing for the Jazz Workshop, his own ensemble founded in the early 1950s, Charles Mingus played acoustic bass with bands led by Louis Armstrong, Red Norvo, Lionel Hampton, and Duke Ellington. Renowned for his fiery behavior and passionate musicality, Mingus brought to his playing and compositions an earthiness and elegance that reflect his Ellingtonian influences. He was an avid experimentalist with two feet rooted in blues and gospel music.
• Mingus Ah Um *(Columbia)*
• Mingus Plays Piano *(Impulse)*

Thelonious Monk
(1917–1982)

Influenced by the great stride pianist James P. Johnson and by pianist-composer Duke Ellington, Monk himself was an American original. With saxophonist Charlie Parker, trumpeter Dizzy Gillespie, and drummer Kenny Clarke, he was one of the creators of bebop. No other pianist can match Monk's sparse, spacious, bluesy-bordering-on-dissonance sound. As a composer, his legacy encompasses numerous jazz standards, including "'Round Midnight," "In Walked Bud," "Straight No Chaser," "Crepuscule with Nellie," "Off-Minor," "Misterioso," and "Monk's Mood."
• The Complete Prestige Recordings
• Genius of Modern Music, *vols. 1 & 2 (Blue Note)*
• Thelonious Monk Plays Duke Ellington *(with Kenny Clarke and Oscar Pettiford: Riverside)*

Joe Morello
(b. 1928)

At the close of 1956 and a three-year gig with pianist Marian McPartland's trio, drummer Joe Morello joined the popular Dave Brubeck Quartet, which was bound for glory. He stayed on for eleven years. Since 1975, when he lost his eyesight, he has been teaching percussion, but blindness hasn't stopped him from performing.
• Time Out *(with the Dave Brubeck Quartet: Columbia/Legacy)*

Esther Morrow
(c. 1943)

Esther Morrow (also known as Esther Marrow and as Queen Esther) is a native of Newport Beach, Virginia. A powerful performer, she made her name when she sang in Duke Ellington's first Sacred Concert at Grace Cathedral in San Francisco in 1966. Subsequently she appeared on Broadway as Aunt Em in *The Wiz*, wrote for and acted in Hollywood films, played Oscar the Grouch's mother on *Sesame Street*, and sang backup for and recorded with Bob Dylan. In 1992 she founded the Harlem Gospel Singers and dubbed herself Queen Esther, and has been quietly touring worldwide ever since.
• *Queen Esther Marrow and the Harlem Gospel Singers*, God Cares *(Chordant)*

Gerry Mulligan
(1927–1996)

While a generation of beatniks may have loved him for the soundtrack he scored for the 1960 Hollywood version of novelist Jack Kerouac's *The Subterraneans*, Gerald Joseph Mulligan, a New Yorker by birth, personified West Coast jazz to the music world in general. Even though he'd been a teenage wonder, contributing arrangements to Gene Krupa's band, and had recorded with Miles Davis (on alto and not his trademark baritone saxophone), it wasn't until the recordings with trumpeter Chet Baker and a piano-less quartet in the early 1950s that Gerry Mulligan first drew popular acclaim and subsequent commercial success. Prized and adored as a player, composer, and arranger, Mulligan left his mark on jazz.
• Gerry Mulligan in Paris *(MCA, 2-CD set)*

105

Ray Nance
(1913–1976)

Not only did he play a mighty cornet and a mean violin, Ray Nance could sing. He's the singer who first put the *doo-wah-doo-wah* into Ellington's scorching remake of "It Don't Mean a Thing (If It Ain't Got That Swing)." Nance jubilantly vocalized the lick he'd heard the horn section riffing. While he was highly regarded and admired for his own horn playing, Nance's violinizing deeply influenced European violinists Stéphane Grappelli and Jean-Luc Ponty, who cite him as an inspiration. Ray will always be lovingly identified with the Ellington Orchestra of the 1940s and 50s, but he also led his own groups and recorded with Grappelli, Earl Hines, and Rosemary Clooney.
• Best of the Complete Duke Ellington RCA Victor Mid-Forties Recordings *(RCA)*

Anita O'Day
(1919–2006)

Anita O'Day (born Anita Belle Colton), above all else, was hip. Plus she had rhythm. When she sang with Gene Krupa, Stan Kenton, and other big bands during the 1940s and 50s, she let the audience know she was no flowery adornment; she was a musician whose instrument was her voice. You can hear her influence on jazz and vernacular singing in the vocal styles of June Christy, Ann Richards, Chris Connor, Mary Ann McCall, and Rickie Lee Jones.
• All the Sad Young Men *(Verve)*

Queen Esther: See Esther Morrow

Daniel Ray: See Big Black

Marshall Royal
(1912–1995)

Marshall Royal was the outstanding lead alto saxophonist in the Count Basie band from the early 1950s through 1970. He also served as "straw boss," taking care of everyday business the Count didn't always have time to handle. Clarity and precision distinguished his sound. The trumpet playing of his brother Ernie Royal was equally esteemed.
• Royal Blue *(Concord Jazz)*

Jimmy Rushing
(1903–1972)

Born into a musical family, James Andrew Rushing could play piano and violin. He knew musical theory, too. "In 1929," Count Basie told jazz biographer Nat Shapiro, "we picked up a blues singer in Oklahoma City. That was Jimmy Rushing, who for my money has never had an equal when it comes to the blues. In all the time he was with the band, Jimmy Rushing has been what I might call my right arm. There were times in the early days of the band that I'd have given it all up but for Jimmy's urging to stick with it." Rushing made his name as a gruff blues shouter with the Basie band, but his tender way with a ballad still haunts listeners.
• Count Basie: The Complete Decca Recordings
• *Dave Brubeck Quartet featuring Jimmy Rushing,* Brubeck & Rushing *(Sony)*

Nina Simone
(1933–2003)

Born Eunice Kathleen Waymon, Nina Simone was recognized early as a talented pianist by patrons in her North Carolina community. Thanks to their support, she was able to study at Juilliard School of Music. Trained in classical music, she began her singing career quite accidentally when her employers at Atlantic City's Midtown Bar and Grill informed her that they expected her to sing as well as play. By 1958 she had recorded "I Love You Porgy," a hit single that ignited her long and sometimes troubled career as a concert performer in the U.S. and Europe. The High Priestess of Soul, as she came to be known, was as socially outspoken as she was passionate about music and everything else.
• Four Women: The Nina Simone Philips Recordings *(Verve, 4-CD set)*

Gabor Szabo
(1936–1982)

Self-taught and daring, Gabor Szabo migrated from Budapest to California during the late 1950s, bringing with him his moody, shimmering sound that was rooted in Hungarian folk and Gypsy music as well as jazz. After studying at Berklee School of Music, he joined the wayward Chico Hamilton Quintet, then played with vibist Gary McFarland. When so-called jazz fusion caught on in the 1970s, Szabo, the

107

...fearless soloist, was poised and ready. He toured and recorded continuously with his own bands and with others, leaving his mark on rock as well as jazz. He died in his hometown.

• *Lena Horne & Gabor Szabo,* Watch What Happens! *(Dcc Compact Classics)*

Muddy Waters
(1915–1983)

McKinley Morganfield is what his parents named him, but Muddy Waters was the name he assumed as one of the most influential of Mississippi's Delta-born blues artists. Waters brought the crying slide and gourdlike thump of the steel-stringed country guitar up to Chicago, where he electrified it. In 1941, folklorist-musicologist Alan Lomax recorded Waters for the Library of Congress. From then on—helped at first by pianist Sunnyland Slim and later working with such original blues artists as Little Walter, Willie Dixon, and Otis Spann—Muddy Waters formed the center of Chicago's postwar blues scene. A string of big-selling records for Chess Records propelled him to international fame.

• The Anthology: 1947–1972 *(MCA)*

Charles "Cootie" Williams
(1910–1985)

"Concerto for Cootie" is how Duke Ellington titled his musical tribute to Charles Melvin Williams, an altogether remarkable trumpet master. Cootie Williams recomposed and pushed the piece to new heights every time he performed it. Williams could make the trumpet growl and purr, whisper and shout, lecture and moan. And when he got his plunger-mute to coax that hypnotic "talking" effect from his horn, Williams was unstoppable and unmatchable.

• *Duke Ellington,* Concerto for Cootie *(RCA)*

Mary Lou Williams
(1910–1981)

A brilliant pianist and arranger, Mary Lou Williams [Mary Elfrieda Scruggs], from the 1920s through the 1970s, was always in style. She gave lessons to bop icons Thelonious Monk and Bud Powell, and she even lived to perform side by side with avant-garde keyboardist Cecil Taylor. Jazz legends Art Tatum and Jelly Roll Morton acknowledged her genius. A self-taught prodigy who began work in vaudeville at the age of six, Williams contributed

arrangements to Andy Kirk's orchestra while she was still in her teens. She went on to write and arrange for Earl Hines, Tommy Dorsey, Benny Goodman, and Duke Ellington.
• My Mama Pinned a Rose on Me *(Pablo)*
• Mary Lou's Mass *(Smithsonian Folkways)*

Eugene Wright
(b. 1923)

Before he made his name internationally during a decade of tenure (1958–1968) with the Dave Brubeck Quartet, Gene Wright, a reconstructed cornet player, had built a reputation for being a bassist you could count on, both metrically and punctually. Before Brubeck he worked with Arnett Cobb, Gene Ammons, Count Basie, and clarinetist Buddy DeFranco. After his stint with Brubeck, he went on world tours with groups of his own, then worked for three years with pianist Monty Alexander.
• *Paul Desmond featuring Jim Hall,* Bossa Antigua *(RCA Victor)*

Joe Zawinul
(1932–2007)

Viennese by birth, Josef Erich Zawinul spent his early childhood playing accordion before studying piano and composition at the Vienna Conservatory. Much of his childhood was spent ducking SS officers during Europe's infamous anti-jazz Nazi era. A survivor, Zawinul first played professionally with Austrian tenor saxophonist Hans Koller before he found his way to the U.S. Following stints with Maynard Ferguson's and Slide Hampton's big bands, he became Dinah Washington's pianist for three years. It was the nine years he spent with Julian Cannonball Adderley's quintet that built his name as a formidable player and composer of soulful jazz standards: "Mercy, Mercy, Mercy," "Country Preacher," and "Walk Tall." After collaborating with Miles Davis on *In a Silent Way,* a landmark album, Zawinul, with saxophonist Wayne Shorter, founded the globally popular Weather Report.
• The Rise and Fall of the Third Stream/ Money in the Pocket *(Rhino)*

Technical Notes

PRACTICALLY SPEAKING, no pictures were done with flash. The Nikon S2 and S3 were my tools of choice. The 35mm and 50mm were the lenses I most often used handheld, sometimes for exposures as low as 1/15 second wide open (f/2.5 and 1.4). For tight head shots with the Nikon F, early on I used the f/4 200mm, and later, to my delight, the then-new f/2.5 180mm, a real beauty for sharpness, contrast, and focus. TRI-X was my film at 650 ASA in D-76. For a short time I used TRI-X in Acufine at 1200 ASA.

Darkroom prints were done in Dektol on Agfa's Brovira paper. I want a cold black tone, some in every print, with a maximum gray scale. The latter is the hardest to achieve.

The images for this book were scanned in the Epson 4870, and edited with Photoshop 6.0. As an editing tool, Photoshop keeps you humble, but it is fantastic for making corrections that might take a lifetime in a wet darkroom—or that might not be possible at all.

I wonder if those just starting out in photography with no wet darkroom experience appreciate the gray scale of black-and-white.

C L R

Further Reading

Ask Me Now: Conversations on Jazz and Literature. Sascha Feinstein, ed. Bloomington: Indiana University Press, 2007.

Beneath the Underdog: His World as Composed by Mingus. Charles Mingus. New York: Knopf, 1971.

Bill Evans: How My Heart Sings. Peter Pettinger. New Haven: Yale University Press, 1998.

Bird: The Legend of Charlie Parker. Robert George Reisner. New York: Bonanza Books, 1962.

Black Beauty, White Heat: A Pictorial History of Classic Jazz. Frank Driggs and Harrison Lewine. New York: William Morrow & Co., 1982.

Black Music in the Harlem Renaissance: A Collection of Essays. Samuel A. Floyd, Jr., ed. New York: Greenwood Press, 1990.

Black Music of Two Worlds. John Storm Roberts. New York: William Morrow & Co., 1974.

Black Music, White Business: Illuminating the History and Political Economy of Jazz. Frank Kofsky. New York: Pathfinder Press, 1998.

Black Talk. Ben Sidran. New York: Holt, Rinehart and Winston, 1971.

Blue Note: Jazz Photography of Francis Wolff. Michael Cuscuna, Charlie Lourie, and Oscar Schnider. New York: St. Martin's Press, 2000.

Broken Spears: A Maasai Journey. Elizabeth L. Gilbert. New York: Grove/Atlantic, 2003.

California Soul: Music of African Americans in the West. Jacqueline Cogdell DjeDje and Eddie S. Meadows, eds. Berkeley: University of California Press, 1998.

Can't Be Satisfied: The Life and Times of Muddy Waters. Robert Gordon. Boston: Little, Brown, 2002.

Celebrating Bird: The Triumph of Charlie Parker. Gary Giddins. New York: William Morrow & Co., 1987.

Celebrating the Duke, and Louis, Bessie, Billie, Bird, Carmen, Miles, Dizzy, and Other Heroes. Ralph J. Gleason. Boston: Little, Brown, 1975.

Clifford Brown: The Life and Art of the Legendary Jazz Trumpeter. Nick Catalano. Oxford and New York: Oxford University Press, 2000.

Conversation with the Blues. Paul Oliver. Cambridge and New York: Cambridge University Press, 1997.

Dance of the Infidels: A Portrait of Bud Powell. Francis Paudras, trans. Rubye Monet. New York: Da Capo Press, 1998.

Duke Ellington: A Listener's Guide. Eddie Lambert. Lanham, Md.: Scarecrow Press, 1999.

Duke Ellington in Person: An Intimate Memoir. Mercer Ellington. New York: Da Capo Press, 1979.

Four Jazz Lives. A. B. Spellman. Ann Arbor: University of Michigan Press, 2004.

The Golden Age of Jazz: On-Location Portraits, in Words and Pictures, of More Than 200 Outstanding Musicians from the Late '30s through the '40s. William P. Gottlieb. New York: Da Capo Press, 1979.

The Great Jazz Day. Charles Graham. Emeryville, Calif.: Woodford Press, 2000.

Half Past Autumn: A Retrospective. Gordon Parks. Boston: Bulfinch Press, 1997.

I Put a Spell on You: The Autobiography of Nina Simone. Nina Simone and Stephen Cleary. Cambridge, Mass.: Da Capo Press, 2003.

Jazz. John Fordham. London and New York: D. Kindersley, 1993.

Jazz: A Photo History. Joachim-Ernst Berendt, trans.

William Odom. New York: Schirmer Books, 1979.

Jazz: The First Century. John Edward Hasse, ed. New York: William Morrow & Co., Inc., 2000.

The Jazz Exiles: American Musicians Abroad. Bill Moody. Reno: University of Nevada Press, 1993.

The Jazz Makers. Nat Shapiro and Nat Hentoff. New York: Grove Press, 1957.

Jazz on the Barbary Coast. Tom Stoddard. Berkeley: Heyday Books, 1998.

Klook: The Story of Kenny Clarke. Mike Hennessey. London: Quartet Books, 1990.

Lester Leaps In: The Life and Times of Lester "Pres" Young. Douglas Henry Daniels. Boston: Beacon Press, 2002.

A Life in Ragtime: A Biography of James Reese Europe. Reid Badger. New York: Oxford University Press, 1995.

Lush Life: A Biography of Billy Strayhorn. David Hajdu. New York: North Point Press, 1997.

The Memphis Blues Again: Six Decades of Memphis Music Photographs. Ernest C. Withers and Daniel Wolff. New York: Viking Studio, 2001.

Miles: The Autobiography. Miles Davis with Quincy Troupe. New York: Simon & Schuster, 1989.

Milestones 1: The Music and Times of Miles Davis to 1960. Jack Chambers. Toronto: University of Toronto Press, 1983.

Milestones 2: The Music and Times of Miles Davis since 1960. Jack Chambers. New York: William Morrow & Co., Inc., 1985.

Mingus Mingus: Two Memoirs. Janet Coleman and Al Young. New York: Limelight Editions, 2004.

Monterey Jazz Festival: Forty Legendary Years. William Minor. Santa Monica, Calif.: Angel City Press, 1997.

Morning Glory: A Biography of Mary Lou Williams. Linda Dahl. Berkeley: University of California Press, 2001.

Music: Black, White and Blue. Ortiz M. Walton. New York: William Morrow & Co., 1972.

Music Is My Mistress: An Autobiography in Three Acts. Duke Ellington. New York: Da Capo Press, 1976.

Notes of a Pianist. Louis Moreau Gottschalk. New York: Knopf, 1964.

Open Sky: Sonny Rollins and His World of Improvisation. Eric Nisenson. New York: St. Martin's Press, 2000.

Pee Wee Russell: The Life of a Jazzman. Robert Hilbert. New York: Oxford University Press, 1993.

Peter Shen's Face Fortunes. Arthur Taylor. New York: Putnam, 1982.

The Poetry of the Blues. Samuel Barclay Charters. New York: Oak Publications, 1963.

Portrait of an Age. Erich Salomon. New York: Collier-Macmillan, 1967.

Queen of the Blues: A Biography of Dinah Washington. James Haskins. New York: William Morrow & Co., 1987.

Raise Up Off Me: A Portrait of Hampton Hawes. Hampton Hawes. New York: Da Capo Press, 1979.

Rat Race Blues: The Musical Life of Gigi Gryce. Noal Cohen and Michael Fitzgerald. Berkeley: Berkeley Hills Books, 2002.

Rhapsodies in Black: Art of the Harlem Renaissance. Richard J. Powell and David A. Bailey, eds. Berkeley: University of California Press, 1997.

Richard Cook's Jazz Encyclopedia. Richard Cook. New York: Penguin, 2006.

Seeing Jazz: Artists and Writers on Jazz. Clark Terry and Milt Hinton. San Francisco: Chronicle Books, 1997.

The Sound of Surprise: 46 Pieces on Jazz. Whitney Balliett. New York: Penguin, 1963.

Straight Life: The Story of Art Pepper. Art Pepper. New York: Da Capo Press, 1994.

Straight, No Chaser: The Life and Genius of Thelonious Monk. Leslie Gourse. New York: Schirmer Books, 1997.

Strange Fruit: The Biography of a Song. David Margolick and Hilton Als. New York: Harper Perennial, 2001.

Swing to Bop: An Oral History of the Transition in Jazz in the 1940s. Ira Gitler. Oxford: Oxford University Press, 1985.

Taj Mahal: Autobiography of a Bluesman. Taj Mahal with Stephen Foehr. London: Sanctuary Press, 2001.

To Be or Not to Bop: The Memoirs of Dizzy Gillespie. Dizzy Gillespie and Al Fraser. Garden City, N.J.: Doubleday & Company, 1979.

The Trouble with Cinderella: An Outline of Identity. Artie Shaw. New York: Farrar, Straus and Young, 1952.

The World of Count Basie. Stanley Dance. New York: C. Scribner's Sons, 1980.

The World of Earl Hines. Stanley Dance. New York: Da Capo Press, 1983.

About the Authors

BORN IN 1933 AND RAISED IN BALTIMORE, Maryland, Charles L. Robinson was educated at California State University at San Francisco, where he earned his Bachelor of Arts degree in Biological Science as well as a Master of Science degree in Vocational Rehabilitation Counseling. His love of jazz and photography date back to childhood. From 1960 to 1969 he worked as a rehabilitation counselor and supervisor for the State of California. At the invitation of Ralph J. Gleason, Robinson also spent some of that time serving the Monterey Jazz Festival as staff photographer. For the next twenty-five years, he worked variously in Oakland, Richmond, and San Francisco as an employment program manager for the State of California.

The father of two, Robinson has devoted his life to community service, almost always as a volunteer. From his graduate school days, when he counseled emotionally disturbed teenagers, to the present, he has served as an advisor to the Oakland Mayor's Summer Jobs Program, as board member and president of the South Berkeley Housing Development Corporation and the Cooperative Center Federal Credit Union, and as lector for St. Joseph the Worker Church. In addition to community development, Robinson's many interests include music appreciation, auto repair, commemorative postage stamps, biographies, and music appreciation. He lives with his wife, Sarah, in Berkeley.

AL YOUNG, BORN IN 1939 AT OCEAN SPRINGS, Mississippi, grew up in Detroit and immigrated to California when he turned twenty. He is the author of more than twenty books of poetry, fiction, and nonfiction. They include the novels *Sitting Pretty; Who Is Angelina?;* and *Seduction by Light*; *Heaven: Poems 1956–1990; The Sound of Dreams Remembered: Poems 1990–2000; Coastal Nights and Inland Afternoons: Poems 2001–2006;* and *Something About the Blues*. With Janet Coleman he coauthored *Mingus Mingus: Two Memoirs*. He is also the editor of *African American Literature: A Brief Introduction and Anthology*. During the 1970s and early 80s he worked as a screenwriter for Sidney Poitier, Bill Cosby, and Richard Pryor. His collections of musical memoirs (*Bodies & Soul, Kinds of Blue, Things Ain't What They Used to Be, Drowning in the Sea of Love*), in which music and memory mix, have been widely praised. A regular contributor of liner notes to Verve's jazz albums, Young has taught writing and literature at Stanford University, UC Santa Cruz, and the University of Michigan. The recipient of Guggenheim, NEA, and Fulbright fellowships, he lives in Berkeley and is Poet Laureate of California.

HEYDAY INSTITUTE

Since its founding in 1974, Heyday Books has occupied a unique niche in the publishing world, specializing in books that foster an understanding of the history, literature, art, environment, social issues, and culture of California and the West. We are a 501(c)(3) nonprofit organization based in Berkeley, California, serving a wide range of people and audiences.

We are grateful for the generous funding we've received for our publications and programs during the past year from foundations and more than three hundred and fifty individual donors. Major supporters include:

Anonymous; Audubon California; BayTree Fund; B.C.W. Trust III; S. D. Bechtel, Jr. Foundation; Fred & Jean Berensmeier; Joan Berman; Book Club of California; Butler Koshland Fund; California State Automobile Association; California State Coastal Conservancy; California State Library; Candelaria Fund; Columbia Foundation; Community Futures Collective; Compton Foundation, Inc.; Malcolm Cravens Foundation; Lawrence Crooks; Judith & Brad Croul; Laura Cunningham; David Elliott; Federated Indians of Graton Rancheria; Fleishhacker Foundation; Wallace Alexander Gerbode Foundation; Richard & Rhoda Goldman Fund; Marion E. Greene; Evelyn & Walter Haas, Jr. Fund; Walter & Elise Haas Fund; Charlene C. Harvey; Leanne Hinton; James Irvine Foundation; Matthew Kelleher; Marty & Pamela Krasney; Guy Lampard & Suzanne Badenhoop; LEF Foundation; Robert Levitt; Dolores Zohrab Liebmann Fund; Michael McCone; National Endowment for the Arts; National Park Service; Philanthropic Ventures Foundation; Alan Rosenus; Mrs. Paul Sampsell; Deborah Sanchez; San Francisco Foundation; William Saroyan Foundation; Melissa T. Scanlon; Seaver Institute; Contee Seely; Sandy Cold Shapero; Skirball Foundation; Stanford University; Orin Starn; Swinerton Family Fund; Thendara Foundation; Susan Swig Watkins; Tom White; Harold & Alma White Memorial Fund; and Dean Witter Foundation.

HEYDAY INSTITUTE BOARD OF DIRECTORS

Michael McCone (chair), Barbara Boucke, Peter Dunckel, Karyn Flynn, Theresa Harlan, Leanne Hinton, Nancy Hom, Susan Ives, Marty Krasney, Guy Lampard, Lee Swenson, Jim Swinerton, Lynne Withey.

For more information about Heyday Institute, our publications and programs, please visit our website at www.heydaybooks.com.

Other BayTree Books

BayTree Books, a project of Heyday Institute,
gives voice to a full range of California experience and personal stories.

Archy Lee: A California Fugitive Slave Case (2008)
Rudolph M. Lapp

Fast Cars and Frybread: Reports from the Rez (2007)
Gordon Johnson

The Oracles: My Filipino Grandparents in America (2006)
Pati Navalta Poblete

Ticket to Exile (2007)
Adam David Miller

Tree Barking: A Memoir (2008)
Nesta Rovina

Walking Tractor: And Other Country Tales (2008)
Bruce Patterson

Where Light Takes Its Color from the Sea: A California Notebook (2008)
James D. Houston

Former railroad sign at Dwight Way in Berkeley